Sorry, We Have No Money

Britain's Economic Problem

By Warwick Lightfoot

First published 2010 by Searching Finance Ltd, 8 Whitehall Road, London W7 2JE, UK

ISBN 978-1-907720-04-8

Book design and typesetting by j-views, Kamakura, Japan

Dedication

WALTER ELTIS, DLITT, EMERITUS FELLOW OF
EXETER COLLEGE, OXFORD

THIS BOOK IS DEDICATED TO WALTER ELTIS for two reasons. One is very personal to me. Walter Eltis was my economics tutor at university. He is a man to whom I owe a great deal not just as a university teacher, but as a person who has been very helpful to me throughout my life. The second reason why I have dedicated this book to him is that it was his work with Robert Bacon in the 1970s, set out in 'Britain's Economic Problem: Too Few Producers' that placed public expenditure and the structural character of the problems that it could create on the public agenda of practical policy makers.

Acknowledgements

THE ANALYSIS IN THIS BOOK draws on and marshals the scholarship and research literature of the international economics community. I would like to thank David Heald and Alison Wolf for allowing me to draw on their research, and Jack Grimston the education correspondent of the *Sunday Times*. I am most grateful to Nick Paget Brown, Clive Tucker and David Stanton for their comments on the book and to Daniel Truscott for statistical research. I would also like to thank Professor David B Smith of the University of Derby, the IFS for the advice and help of its economists, the statisticians at the ONS and the OECD.

Sorry, We Have No Money

Britain's Economic Problem

By Warwick Lightfoot

About the author

WARWICK LIGHTFOOT IS A PROFESSIONAL ECONOMIST with specialist interests in monetary policy, public expenditure, taxation and labour markets.

Formerly the economics editor of *The European*, he was for many years a frequent contributor to the *Wall Street Journal* and has written for the *Financial Times*, *The Times*, the *Sunday Times*, the *Daily Telegraph*, the *Sunday Telegraph*, and the *Guardian*. His articles on economics and public policy have also been published in specialist journals that range from *Financial World*, *International Economy*, and the *Investors Chronicle* to the *Times Literary Supplement* and the *Journal of Insolvency Practitioners*.

Warwick worked in UK government as Special Adviser to the Chancellor of the Exchequer from 1989-92, initially appointed by Nigel Lawson and later reappointed by John Major and Norman Lamont. He was also Special Adviser to the Secretary of State for Employment, the Rt Hon Norman Fowler MP. He is a Councillor in the Royal Borough of Kensington and Chelsea.

About Searching Finance Ltd

SEARCHING FINANCE LTD is a dynamic new voice in financial services, business and economics. Our mission is to provide expert, highly relevant and actionable comment, information and analysis. We bring you the latest industry insight and best practice guidance, provided by writers who are renowned experts in their field, to give you the knowledge that will gain an edge for you and your organisation. To learn more, please visit www.searchingfinance.co.uk

Contents

Sorry, We Have No Money

Part 2: Capitalism, market limits, state failure and an over-expanded state

Contents

Figures and Tables

Sorry, We Have No Money

Introduction

IN MAY 2010 the Chief Secretary to the Treasury of the incoming Coalition govenment found a note left by his predecessor, stating 'I'm afraid there is no money.' This may have been done in a spirit of good humour but the underlying message could not have been more serious. The UK economy faces a series of connected structural challenges. The fundamental challenge is the long-term one of maintaining and expanding an internationally competitive private sector that will provide the economy and tax base to finance a generous welfare state. A welfare state, moreover, that is being made progressively more expensive, as a result of an ageing population. The UK has a large public sector that is inefficient and imposes both a tax and a regulatory burden that hinders the supply performance of the economy. The public sector does this by blunting the price signals that are at the heart of a properly functioning market economy. It tries to do too much and fails in the process efficiently to carry out those public sector and welfare functions that are critical for the proper functioning of a modern society and an efficient market economy.

These structural economic challenges in turn create acute social and regional geographical problems. They result in many households being locked into permanent cycles of poverty. Individuals, communities and complete regions of the country have become detached from the international market place. These communities and regions exhibit such high levels of public sector activity and such discrete and constrained levels of private or fully market-based activity that the only sensible point of comparison is with the former socialist economies in Central and Eastern Europe or with the East German *Länder* in post-unification Germany. At the heart of these structural problems is the level of public expenditure combined with continued entrenched trade union power, along with producer interests in the public sector that raise the costs and damage the efficiency of the British public sector. Moreover, more than thirty years of attempts to reform the public sector have if anything exposed the entrenched nature of the public sector's low productivity and in some cases aggravated it. The credit crunch, the rescue of the banks and the slump in output between 2008 and 2009 have exposed the vulnerability of the UK economy and aggravated these long-term structural problems. They have also created an immediate crisis in the public finances that has to be addressed not only to stabilise the public finances in the short term, but to contain the longer-term structural challenges that the UK economy faces.

There are two fundamental propositions that inform this book. The first is that successful modern societies and market economies need a significant and efficiently functioning public sector, providing public goods and also a broader range of public services that are best provided on a collective basis. The second proposition is that public spending involves costs that go beyond the simple cash cost, because the taxes needed to pay for it impose a deadweight cost on the economy. It is therefore very important to ensure that 'at the margin' public spending does not rise beyond the point where it generates clear benefits in excess of its costs. Diminishing marginal returns mean that at some point, public spending imposes costs on the economy that exceed its benefits. It is not clear what the particular ratio of public spending should be in relation to national income. It probably lies somewhere between 30 and 35 per cent of GDP. Where the tipping point is precisely is difficult to identify. What is clear, however, is that spending in excess of 35 per cent of GDP is higher than the level where the benefits will be greater than its full costs. And a public spending ratio that is decisively above 40 per cent should be reduced.

The structural problems that result when public spending is expanded beyond the point where it yields economic and social benefits that are greater than its full costs became apparent in the UK in the 1960s, when government spending began to absorb more than a third of national income. By the 1970s the structural consequences of a tax burden that descends a long way down the earnings distribution became plain, so that people both pay tax and claim means-tested social security benefits. The inflationary risks of high levels of public spending partly financed through high levels of government borrowing were also revealed. From 1976 the Labour government of James Callaghan started to stabilise the UK public finances with the assistance of the IMF. The Conservative governments of Margaret Thatcher and John Major, as well stabilising the public finances, addressed many of the structural problems in the UK's product and labour markets. Yet the core supply performance issue of a public sector that was too large in relation to national income and entrenched by powerful public sector producer interest groups remained.

Between 1997 and 2010 there was a huge and sustained increase in public spending in cash, real terms and in relation to GDP. In 2010 the level of public spending in relation to national income was returned to the levels of the economic crisis of the mid-1970s, with an even higher budget deficit. Some of the spending and borrowing could be put down to the slump in output between 2008 and 2009 that reduced GDP by 6.4 per cent. The greater share of both the higher spending and borrowing, however, was the result of discretionary decisions to raise public spending across government departments with the exception of defence. These decisions have created public finances that are unsustainable in terms of the level of borrowing and have significantly aggravated the UK's long-term structural public expenditure problem.

An over-expanded public sector will fail to deliver results for the amount of resources being deployed and will retard the economy's rate of growth compared to what it would otherwise achieve. The result will be that in the longer term the state will absorb a larger share of a lower level of national income and GDP per capita will be lower as a result. The UK has over-expanded its public sector at the start of the 21st century, when it faces the twin challenges of paying for an older population and competing with dynamic economies such as Brazil, India and China. The UK needs to nurture an expanding private sector to provide the tax base to finance its ageing community, at a time when its private sector will encounter increasing international competition. A large public sector raises the economy's cost base and has a particularly pronounced effect on the internationally traded part of the economy that will be exposed to this greater competition.

Between 1997 and 2010 the UK government took more money from the private sector and allocated more to the public sector. It took resources from the most productive part of the economy and allocated greater amounts to the least productive part. Apart from the implications that such policies have for the supply performance of the economy, this increase in public spending has yielded few identifiable benefits comparable to the scale of increased resources being employed by the public sector.

Public sector spending rose, yet in the areas that benefited the most the evidence in terms of results and productivity look ambiguous at best, and poor on a realistic assessment. The ONS has investigated the results of increased spending carefully and its research shows that higher spending on areas such as health, education and social services was not matched by comparable increases in output, but by a smaller increase in output than the resources spent, combined with a fall in public sector productivity.

This disappointing use of resources by the UK public sector is interesting because since the late 1970s the UK public sector has been subject to a succession of policy initiatives and structural changes to improve its efficiency. Among them are cash limits, Lord Rayner's Whitehall efficiency scrutinies, contracting out, the creation of purchaser/provider splits within a quasi-market structure or internal market in the NHS and the private finance initiative. These were often in themselves worthwhile – although some, like the private finance initiative, have been expensive and damaging. These attempts at reform were not able to overcome the inherent problem in the public sector that people spending other peoples' money are not as careful with it as they are with their own because they do not have an incentive to behave in a comparably efficient manner.

Sorry, We Have No Money

On occasions the reforms simply changed the locus or framework in which inefficiency occurs. A good example is contracting out, where the point of inefficiency becomes the tendering process for the contract, where over-specification, complexity, perverse incentives and lack of proper attention to detail simply offer an alternative framework for rent seeking, with the private sector replacing public sector direct labour organisations.

A distinguishing feature of UK public sector reform is that it has been a managerial response to clear and obvious inefficiency that arises out of the interaction of public sector trade union power and national collective pay bargaining arrangements. Instead of confronting the matters that are at the heart of the efficiency problem in the public sector, reforms often have been an elaborate exercise in trying to step around them without actually addressing the problem that needs to be sorted. Not only have public sector managers failed to confront the central factors that make the direct provision and management of their services expensive and inefficient, they have lacked the confidence and will-power to manage their services properly within the present pay and bargaining arrangements. Where there is flexibility and discretion it has tended to be used to accommodate higher pay rather than to contain costs.

There are no easy wins in the agenda of the public service reform that needs to be pursued in the UK. Unlike the 1970s, there are no extensive food and production subsidies that can simply be ended, or nationalised industries to return to proper management and profit. Public spending today largely goes on things that the state needs to be involved in. The questions that need to be looked at are how much should be spent and how well is the cost base being controlled. The cost base largely turns on the level of public sector pay and pensions. The overall level of affordability turns on public sector pay and pensions, along with the level of social security transfer payments. It should be possible to reduce the public sector spending share of national income to around 35 per cent of GDP, by taking a further 2 percentage points of GDP out of the public sector pay and pensions bill and 2 percentage points of GDP out of the social security budget, over and above the public expenditure plans outlined in the Coalition's Emergency Budget in June 2010.

Simply removing the structural budget deficit, which is the heart of the Coalition's present fiscal strategy, is insufficient. Reducing public spending from over 47 per cent to just under 40 per cent would represent a significant and beneficial rebalancing of the UK economy. It is not, however, enough; a public sector that absorbs around two fifths of national income will result in a tax burden that travels a long way down the earnings distribution. The full costs of the spending will not be matched by benefits that exceed those costs. The central issue that Robert Bacon and Walter Eltis raised in 'Britain's Economic Problem: Too Few Producers' (1976) would remain. Moreover, the character of the problem has changed and become more challenging over the last thirty years. The public sector imposes a cost on the private sector and makes it harder for the private sector to compete in markets at home and abroad where it faces competitive challenge. Today, that international competitive challenge is now much greater. Its scale if anything is probably underestimated.

The present budget deficit is unsustainable and its structural or permanent element needs to be eliminated. An undue focus on the present level of government borrowing and the stock of public debt may, however, distract attention from the central long-term structural problem that the UK has of reducing public spending rather than concentrating on the secondary matter of how it is financed between borrowing and taxation. Borrowing has a legitimate function in emergencies such as war, smoothing the cost of expensive capital projects – that are properly costed – over generations and stimulating demand and output during slumps after an adverse economic shock. Historically, a liquid and deep government debt market has been of great convenience to households, insurance companies and pension funds. There is, however, a cost to government borrowing and a large stock of government debt

Sorry, We Have No Money

makes the operation of monetary policy more complicated; this may in the future raise the long-term cost of borrowing and reduce future capital investment and productive capacity. The Coalition government is right to address the level of UK borrowing because there was a genuine danger that the government was starting to have peacetime public finances where the scale of permanent borrowing and the level of debt would invite the kind of fundamental questions about the UK's credibility as a borrower that would make economic management more difficult and expensive.

The credit crunch and banking crisis resulted in what some economists have called the 'Great Recession' and others have called the 'Second Great Contraction'. The slump in output in 2008 and 2009 along with the financial crisis, caused some people to question the fundamentals of a market-based economy. And there is no doubt that some people believed that there would be a return to a more managed economy with a much greater role for the public sector. Part 2 of this book tries to explore why this is unlikely and touches on the fundamentals of capitalism, how it has historically worked as a social phenomenon and yielded huge benefits in terms of living standards. It tries to show how markets can only function properly if they are rooted in a wider context of law, regulation and social institutions.

It also tries to explore and summarise some of the fundamental theoretical issues that determine the balance between the public and private sectors and why there is a general presumption that goods and services should be produced in private, competitive markets. It looks at some of the fundamental propositions of the neo-classical economic framework, and in doing so explores the circumstances where markets fail and need to be supplemented by extensive state intervention. This part of the book benefited greatly from David Heald's survey of these issues, who as well as setting out the conditions for market failure shows how efforts to correct it can also result in state failure. In many respects, much of the thinking of socialist economists in the first half of the 20th century was

Introduction

an attempt to overcome that sort of state failure or inefficiency in planning, through the use of things such quasi markets and shadow prices. These have often been the devices that public sector policy makers have turned to when attempting to improve the performance of the public sector over the last twenty years.

For many people, the great counter-factual to any proposition that public spending should be limited to 35 or even 40 per cent of national income is the so-called Nordic model and Sweden in particular. There are many attractive and admirable things about Scandinavia, not least its success in maintaining democratic institutions in the darkest days of the 20th century, the rule of law and the probity of its public service. Yet the picture painted, particularly of Sweden, as a society able to combine very high standards of living with an usually large public sector is misleading. The final chapter of this book looks at Sweden. It shows the unusual and distinctive features of Sweden's economic evolution, how much of its success is more appropriately attributed to elements such as its openness to international trade than to its level of public spending, how slow in fact Sweden was to increase state spending compared to other OECD economies and how, when it did, problems began to accumulate. In 1970, Sweden's GDP per capita was about 10 per cent lower than that in the US. After the Swedish model's crisis in the 1990s GDP per capita fell relative to the US and ended up 25 per cent lower. The circumstances that enabled the Swedish model to flourish were particular – in the 1990s it became unstable and foundered. In terms of inter-generational social mobility, Sweden lags behind other advanced OECD economies. Rather than being an exemplar of how things could be done differently, Sweden offers an example of the costs that a large public sector imposes on an economy.

The implications of the analysis presented here are optimistic. The conclusions of this book are that a public sector that is large by historic standards yields genuine economic and social benefits. A welfare state and a public sector that carefully mitigate market

Sorry, We Have No Money

failure, far from damaging the operation of a market economy, help it to flourish. The challenge is an empirical and practical one of achieving a balance between a public sector that provides services that people need and supports the functioning of the private sector. The judgment about that balance needs to be realistic in appreciating that it is the market sector that ultimately has to finance the state though taxation. The challenge in the UK and throughout most of the OECD, is to reduce the level of public expenditure as a share of national income to a level that harnesses the benefits of public intervention in a way that is consistent with nurturing the private sector. It is an expanding private or market sector that will generate the tax base, which will finance the kind of social services that we will want and will increasingly need in an ageing society.

Introduction

Part 1
Britain's structural economic problem: Public expenditure and economic performance

Chapter 1: Britain's supply-side challenge in the 21st century

The need for a strong public sector

MODERN MARKET ECONOMIES need significant public sectors if they are to function efficiently. Markets need a secure institutional framework of law, regulation and competition rules if they are to function properly. That has been the clear lesson from the transition economies in Central and Eastern Europe that have embarked on the process of establishing market economies following the collapse of Communism in 1989. Successful market economies also flourish best when there is a clear appreciation of the need for substantial public intervention to balance the imperfections that markets exhibit.

Public goods

TRADITIONALLY THE STATE WAS SEEN as necessary for providing certain narrow public goods that markets could not easily provide. These normally were things such as street lighting, lighthouses, defence and criminal justice. Modern states rightly take on a much wider range of activities that go far beyond this narrow range. Governments collectively organise and finance many services that could be done by private individuals or firms where there are either disproportionate costs to market provision or where low income households would be unable to access the goods and services that they need. The wide dispersion of income and wealth that market economies exhibit requires collective action by governments to ensure that all households have access to minimum standards of income and welfare. In modern societies collective action by governments is an important part of ensuring both efficient markets and an optimal outcome in terms of individual living standards and welfare.

A welfare state that goes beyond narrow public goods

MODERN STATES INTERVENE in a range of ways.

As well as providing classic public goods they provide services such as education, health and pensions ('merit goods'). These services could in principle be organised and paid for privately, but the public interest in having them provided at an adequate level for all households results in government intervention. Not all households value education; however, because of the wider public interest in an educated society the state compels parents to send their children to school. Given that many parents, who value education, are neither in the position to organise it nor pay for it for their own children, the state organises it and pays for it. Insurance markets exhibit limitations that prevent some people from obtaining insurance cover for certain important risks or only make it available at a disproportionate cost. These are the reasons that governments intervene in the provision of health care and also provide it for households that could in principle pay for it themselves. Likewise, governments provide basic and earnings-related pensions to help low income households and average income households accumulate long-term savings and pension assets at a reasonable cost. Much of what the state does through collective provision is to assist people to smooth their incomes over the life cycle. Households get given cash when they have children and money is often scarce. Tax tends to be levied on them in middle age when their earnings are highest and their family responsibilities are lighter. And benefits are paid out in pensions, health care and other services provided in old age when incomes are limited.

As these welfare services have been developed over the last century there has been a huge improvement in a whole range of economic and social indicators throughout the advanced OECD economies. Britain was in many respects in the vanguard of the development of the comprehensive welfare state. The wartime coalition government led by Winston Churchill put in place its principal building blocks by accepting the recommendations of the Beveridge Report that built on national insurance legislation passed in 1909. The 1944 Butler Education Act established the framework for post-war state education. The final building block was the National Health Service, established by the Attlee Labour government in 1948. As a result of these measures Britain constructed a comprehensive welfare state. The term welfare state appears to have been coined by the Archbishop of Canterbury in a wartime BBC radio broadcast. It would, as Churchill vividly described it, offer people support from the 'cradle to the grave'. Having expanded publicly funded arts provision for the general public during the war, the Churchill Coalition government set up the Arts Council, initially chaired by Lord Keynes. This explicitly recognised that there was a role for the state in subsidising the arts, acting both as a patron and to make the arts available to a much wider public than had previously been the case.

Britain may have been in the vanguard, but it was not alone among advanced economies in establishing a comprehensive welfare state. Some countries, notably Germany, if anything have an older and more developed tradition of social insurance than Britain. In the 1950s and 1960s generous welfare states were created throughout the advanced OECD economies. This process transformed the role of governments in the social and economic lives of their citizens. Levels of public expenditure and tax burdens that once would only have been tolerated for brief periods of wartime emergency became the peacetime normality.

Efficient and extensive welfare states can improve the functioning of market economies

TWO ECONOMISTS HAVE CATALOGUED this international process.

Vito Tanzi and Ludger Schuknecht have had the advantage of having worked on fiscal policy at the IMF. Indeed for many years Tanzi was the Director of the IMF's Fiscal Affairs Unit. Their book 'Public Spending in the 20th Century: a Global Perspective' (2000) sets out the secular rise in the ratio of state spending to national income clearly.

- ❑ In 1913 public spending accounted for about 13 per cent of GDP in industrial economies. In Germany it was 14 per cent and in Britain and the United States it was 12.7 and 7.5 per cent.

- ❑ In the inter-war years from 1918 to 1939, public expenditure rose sharply. Countries were starting to adopt embryonic social insurance schemes, but the principal driver of higher spending was the impact of the Great Depression. In Britain there was a big expansion of state aid to industries and regions affected by the slump of the 1920s. In America, New Deal programmes which included the establishment of the Social Security pension system hugely expanded the role of the Federal government. In France the Popular Front government in 1936 expanded a whole range of social entitlements, while in Germany and Italy there were unusual experiments in autarky and state direction of the economy along with re-armament spending that significantly increased state expenditure. By 1937 the average ratio of public expenditure to GDP had risen to 23.6 per cent from 19.6 per cent after the end of the First World War. In America it was 19.6 per cent, France 29 per cent, Britain 30 per cent and Germany 34 per cent.

- ❑ In the quarter of the century that followed the end of the Second World War in 1945 the establishment of comprehensive welfare states led to a further significant increase in the role of the state. In 1960 the average ratio of state spending to GDP was 28 per cent. In America it was 27 per cent, Britain 32.8 per cent and in Germany and France 34.6 per cent and 32.4 per cent.

- ❑ Between 1960 and 1980 the average ratio rose more than a quarter by almost 13 percentage points to 41.9 per cent. And between 1980 and 1996 it rose further to 45 per cent.

Tanzi and Schuknecht show that the increases in spending

Sorry, We Have No Money

between 1913 and 1960 yielded real improvements in a variety of social and economic indicators. Their conclusion is clear:

'For the period up to 1960, a reasonable claim can be made that the increased public sector spending (on education, health, training, basic social security, and so on) had led to measurable improvements in economic and social indicators.'

However, the further significant rise in public expenditure after 1960 has yielded little. They conclude that:

'Progress in improving the social and economic objectives slowed down considerably or even reversed in spite of a continuous large expansion in public spending in many countries.'

There are diminishing returns to welfare spending

THIS SIGNIFICANCE OF THE TANZI AND SCHUKNECHT RESEARCH is twofold:

- First, that a historically large public sector providing comprehensive welfare services, in a generous manner, helps a generally free economy to work better.
- Second, that there is a balance. If governments spend much more than a third of GDP they will achieve little in terms of improved social outcomes and the costs will impose burdens that will diminish both economic performance and may also yield some negative social outcomes. Their conclusion is that higher levels of public spending 'impose obvious costs on the tax payer and on the economy, costs that do not seem to be compensated by a better performance in terms of socioeconomic indicators'.

Tanzi and Schuknecht therefore argue that countries should aim to reduce public spending to around 30 per cent of GDP. They propose 30 per cent as a purely indicative figure and accept that different countries will want to make different choices about the precise level of spending that reflects their particular circumstances.

Britain's supply-side challenge in the 21st century

They believe that governments should be able to accomplish much of what can be achieved through public spending within a rough range from 25 per cent to 35 per cent of GDP. Different countries will have different appetites for the collective provision of goods and services reflecting different traditions and cultural values, Tanzi and Schuknecht believe that governments, however, should be able to accomplish what they need to do to accommodate those choices within that range. Given, for example, Britain's history, international role and attachment to institutions, such as the NHS, BBC and Arts Council, a sensible rule of thumb would therefore be to aim to hold the ratio of public expenditure to an average of 35 per cent of GDP over the economic cycle.

Deadweight cost of public expenditure

PUBLIC EXPENDITURE IMPOSES A COST on an economy. That cost is greater than the cash spending involved, because public expenditure allocates resources outside the framework of the price mechanism. Both the spending itself and the taxes raised to finance it distort resource allocation in the economy. Expenditure has to be paid for in the long run by taxes and taxation imposes a deadweight cost on the economy. This means that the cost in terms of economic output lost in the private sector is greater than just the money or revenue raised through taxation to pay for it. Some forms of taxation are more distorting than others. Taxes on income, capital and trade appear to distort the economy more than taxes on expenditure. Government borrowing is effectively delayed taxation. The borrowing itself will also impose costs on an economy by competing for investors' funds in the bond markets and, other things being equal, raising interest rates. The extent to which government deficits raise interest rates will depend on the scale of borrowing in relation to other borrowers and how open international capital markets are. In terms of understanding the cost or impact of public expenditure on an economy, it is important to appreciate that the crucial issue is the

Sorry, We Have No Money

total proportion of national income that is taken and spent by the state. How that level of expenditure is financed between taxation and borrowing is a second order issue.

For many years US policy makers have taken account of the notion of deadweight in framing and costing US public expenditure programmes. In the 1960s economists in the US became interested in trying to measure the deadweight losses that taxation imposed on the US economy. In 1964 Arnold Harberger, who started this area of economic analysis, estimated that income taxes imposed welfare losses of 2.5 per cent of tax revenue raised. More recent American studies have arrived at much larger estimates of deadweight losses. The Congressional Budget Office reports that 'typical estimates of the economic cost of a dollar of tax revenue range from 20 cents to 60 cents over and above the revenue raised'. The Office of Management and Budget employs a 25 per cent deadweight loss assumption when it carries out cost benefit analysis on federal government spending programmes. OMB's rules require that each additional dollar of tax revenue is scored as a cost of $1.25, because taxes 'create an excess burden that is a net loss to society'. This means that a new spending proposal should generate benefits that are at least 25 per cent greater than the explicit financing costs involved.

Discussion of the deadweight consequences of taxation or the 'excess burden' of taxation as it is sometimes referred to, is at the heart of the US policy debate. For example, the President's Council of Economic Advisers in their Economic Report to the President in 2005 devoted a significant part of their analysis to the effects of this on economic behaviour. The report describes how taxation of savings and income distorts economic behaviour and results in the inefficient use of the resources that leads to reductions in economic welfare that can exceed the amount of tax collected. These 'costs above and beyond the revenues collected are called the "excess burden" of the tax system'. The level of distortion to economic decisions and the extent of the excess burden reflect the complexity of the tax system and the level of marginal tax rates.

Britain's supply-side challenge in the 21st century

Public spending and economic growth

THERE COMES A POINT WHEN PUBLIC EXPENDITURE RISES in relation to national income and the benefits are more than offset by the economic costs, with the result that economic growth begins to slow down. Many economists have looked at the connection between increased public spending and the long-term evolution of an economy's capacity to increase output and welfare. The economic literature establishes the proposition that relatively high public spending slows economic growth.

Robert Barro, an economist at Harvard University, has taken a particular interest in economic growth, and in the development of 'new growth theory'. He has estimated that, other things being equal, higher public spending will reduce economic growth and that an additional 1 percentage point increase in the share of government spending in GDP is associated with a 0.14 per cent reduction of GDP growth per head. Barro's estimates corroborate work done by British economist David Smith in the 1970s. These estimates suggest that the increase in public expenditure since 1997 may have reduced per capita GDP growth by between 0.5 and over 1 per cent per year. David Smith has shown that over time that the opportunity cost of the output foregone accumulates into significant missed opportunities. Smith estimates that across the OECD over 45 years the lost output could be as high as 160 per cent. It would be misleading to mechanically assume some simple causation between public expenditure growth and precise rates of GDP growth. Yet the connection is clear. At a certain point the benefits of collective provision of goods and services are exceeded by their costs and this results in a reduced economic performance and losses of economic welfare in the medium term.

Two IMF economists, Gerwin Bell and Norikazu Tawara, looked again at these issues in 'The Size of Government and US-European Differences in Economic Performance', an IMF paper published in 2009. They examine why European economies have over the last thirty years made little progress in closing the gap between their

Sorry, We Have No Money

per capita GDP and that of the US. They look at the distorting effects of taxation on things like labour supply. They are careful to refute the blanket claim that differences in the size of government account for all of the differences in output and labour supply. They conclude, however, that 'the size of government does play a significant role in explaining lower European labour supply, while the size of European governments appears to imply large welfare costs. They found there are large potential welfare gains to be made from 'cutting back government'. For example, using data for 1992–2001 they found that for the UK a cut in marginal tax rates of five percentage points would have increased welfare gains equivalent to 4 per cent of aggregate consumption or 8 per cent if the UK had adopted US tax levels accompanied by offsetting changes in government spending.

The 35 per cent rule of thumb

GIVEN THE FULL COST OF PUBLIC EXPENDITURE and the deadweight cost of taxation, it is therefore very important that public expenditure should yield benefits that exceed its full cost. This is particularly important in relation to spending at the margin. The message from the Tanzi and Schuknecht research is that when the average ratio of public spending was around one-third of GDP it yielded clear and measurable social and economic benefits. But once that point was reached their research implies that additional spending appeared to yield costs that were greater than the benefits. This would suggest that as a rule of thumb governments should aim to keep the ratio of public expenditure at around 35 per cent of national income. By historical standards 35 per cent of GDP would be considered a large public sector. It is slightly higher than the optimal ratio suggested by Tanzi and Schuknecht's research, which suggests that if spending rises much further the cost-to-benefit ratio would become more disappointing.

Britain's supply-side challenge in the 21st century

Britain passed 35 per cent in the 1960s

IN BRITAIN BY THE 1950S a fully functioning developed welfare state was in place. The cost implications had always been recognised by the British Treasury. The wartime Chancellor of the Exchequer, Sir Kingsley Wood, briefed Churchill that the 1942 Beveridge Plan would increase taxation by 30 per cent and warned that 'the weekly progress of the millionaire to the post office for his old age pension would have an element of farce but for the fact that it is to be provided in large measure by the general taxpayer'. Even literary London was realistically appraised of these costs. Dame Rebecca West, who favoured the creation of the welfare state and the NHS, was alarmed at its expense, commenting in 1949 that it is 'as staggering as the cost of war'. While Dame Muriel Spark acidly caricatured the generosity of the 1950s NHS in her novel 'Memento Mori'. It was plain that by 1960 Britain had a comprehensive welfare state with a high ratio of public spending to GDP and a matching tax burden.

Britain's public expenditure crisis in the 1970s

PUBLIC EXPENDITURE FELL from a peak of over 48 per cent of GDP in the mid-1970s, but was never reduced much below 40 per cent on a sustained basis. New Labour's rapid increase in spending in both cash and real terms has resulted in a ratio of public spending to national income comparable to the position in the fiscal crisis in the 1970s. If anything, the Treasury's numbers presented in Figure 1.1 understate the ratio of public spending within national income, because they are expressed in relation to GDP measured at market prices rather than basic prices or factor cost. This means that national income is inflated by indirect taxes. The OECD presents UK public spending some 2 percentage points higher than the Treasury. The OECD also uses market prices and the difference appears to arise because it applies international accounting conventions about

Sorry, We Have No Money

public sector pensions more rigorously than the Treasury and may treat EU transactions differently. The spending plans set out in the Coalition's Emergency Budget in June 2010 project a reduction in the ratio of public spending to national income to around 40 per cent of national income.

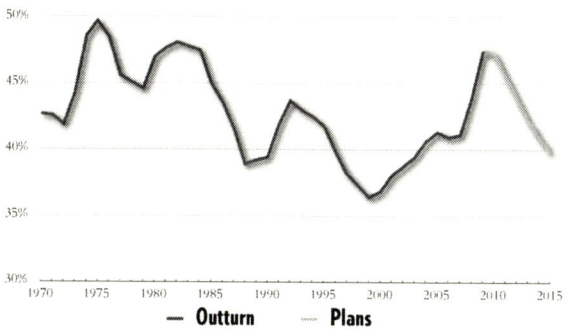

FIGURE 1.1: *Total managed expenditure as a percentage of GDP (Source: HM Treasury)*

Public expenditure continued to rise in the 1960s and 1970s. This partly reflected the working out of the full implications of spending programmes agreed in the 1940s, but it also reflected discretionary changes that extended the scope of public provision in the 1960s. By the mid-1970s it was plain that the UK had a public expenditure problem and a supply performance problem. The 1976 Public Expenditure White Paper set out the position concisely in its introductory page.

'In managing public expenditure two problems stand out. The first has been with us for many years. Popular expectations for improved public services and welfare programmes have not been matched by the growth in output – or by willingness to forgo improvements in private living standards in favour of those programmes. The oil crisis intensified this gap between expectations and available resources. The second problem is that of cost inflation, which has become acute in the last few years, and has added an extra dimension of difficulty.

'In the last three years public expenditure has grown by nearly 20 per cent in volume, while output has grown by less than 2 per cent. The ratio of public expenditure to gross domestic product has risen from 50 per cent to 60 per cent. Fifteen years ago it was 42 per cent. The tax burden has also increased. In 1975-76 a married man on average earnings is paying about a quarter of his earnings in income tax, compared with a tenth in 1960-61. At two-thirds average earnings, he is paying about a fifth compared to less than a twentieth.

'Tax thresholds have fallen sharply in relation to average earnings, and people are being drawn into tax at income levels which are below social security benefit levels. The increase in the tax burden has fallen heavily on low wage earners. Those earning less than the average contribute to over a quarter of the income tax yield. This cannot be made good simply by increasing the burden at the top: if no taxpayer were left with more than £5.00 per annum after tax, this would increase the yield by only 6 per cent.'

Britain's public finances in the 1970s were shambolic. There was a very high ratio of public expenditure to GDP and despite a steadily rising tax burden a budget deficit of 9 per cent of GDP. The management of these difficult public finances was further compounded by high and unstable inflation, a chronic balance of payments problem and periodic sterling crises. This awkward conjunction of separate but related difficulties resulted in the UK having to seek the assistance of the IMF in 1976. The UK received the largest loan that the IMF had made during its history. A loan so large that it had to be facilitated by the US and West German governments. IMF conditionality attached to the loan resulted in significant cuts in public expenditure and to a reduction in the budget deficit. Those measures resolved the crisis and the Callaghan and Thatcher administrations went on to stabilise both the public finances and the economy more broadly.

The 1976 Public Expenditure White Paper, however, set out the

Sorry, We Have No Money

broader and in many ways more intractable structural consequences of a very large public sector. In the 1980s, although public expenditure fell as a ratio of GDP and the budget deficit was transformed into a surplus, the tax burden actually rose. While marginal tax rates were reduced decisively at the top end of the earnings distribution, the structural problems highlighted by the 1976 White Paper meant that much less progress was made in dealing with the established unemployment and poverty traps at the lower end of the earnings distribution. In short, the difficult questions identified by the White Paper have never been resolved. At best in the 1980s and 1990s they were only mitigated.

Britain's fundamental problem: too few producers

TWO ACADEMIC OXFORD ECONOMISTS, Robert Bacon and Walter Eltis, captured the challenges faced by the British economy in the 1970s in an arresting piece of contemporary economic analysis, 'Britain's Economic Problem: Too Few Producers' (1976). The Bacon-Eltis thesis was straightforward:

- From 1961 Britain had shifted resources out of the production of marketable goods and services into non-marketable public services;
- This had reduced the rate of growth and weakened the balance of payments;
- Reduced investment along with the reduced rate of growth constrained the capacity of the economy to provide productive jobs.

Bacon and Eltis offered a structural analysis of the economic consequences of a large public sector that in practice crowds out the private marketable sector. They identified a crowding out problem that emerged in the 1960s and 1970s. Whereas at the time these problems were regarded as no more than disappointing economic growth and a chronic balance of payments constraint. Bacon and

Eltis saw the crowding out starting to emerge after 1960 when public expenditure, having risen rapidly in peacetime during the 1950s, started to increase beyond a third of national income. They also looked at other OECD economies, such as parts of the US and Canada, and suggested that that in the 1970s they were beginning to experience similar problems to Britain's as a result of expanding non-market sectors.

Bacon and Eltis originally set out their argument in a series of articles in the *Sunday Times* in 1975. They not only caught the mood of the moment but captured the interest of the commentators and politicians across the political spectrum. In 1975 inflation touched 25 per cent, there was a budget deficit of 9 per cent and public expenditure was 49 per cent of GDP. In the autumn of 1976, despite a broadly floating exchange rate, there was a full blown sterling crisis as deep and profound as any in the post-war period. Their analysis, while framed in terms of a neo-Keynesian macroeconomic model, challenged the conventional wisdom that had informed economic policy in the post-war period that rising unemployment could be overcome if there was a sufficient increase in public spending.

Their central proposition was that:

❑ The extra public spending would need to be financed by higher taxation;

❑ Higher taxation would result in trade unions using their power in the workplace to raise wages to offset the higher taxes;

❑ The resulting increased employment costs would cause private sector employers to shed labour and become reluctant to invest in future employment-creating capacity;

❑ In order to find work for the displaced private sector workers, public spending has to rise again so that the state can take on the role of employer of last resort, which raises taxes further and aggravates an already malign cycle.

A distinctive feature of the Bacon-Eltis thesis was the structural approach that it took. They distinguished between the tax-financed public sector and the sector that pays the taxes. In the 1970s the nationalised industries accounted for around 10 per cent of market output. Bacon and Eltis therefore divided the economy into the non-market and the market sectors. The market sector included the nationalised industries which in principle made a return on capital and helped to pay for the public sector. Until the Bacon-Eltis thesis, mainstream economists did not take a structural approach to economic analysis. This feature of their analysis was highlighted by Robert Skidelsky, in his foreword to the twentieth anniversary edition of Bacon and Eltis in 1996. Structural pathologies had until then been very much the preserve of Marxist and neo-Marxist economists.

This significant intellectual innovation was largely the result of Walter Eltis's interest in classical growth theory and his work on the 18th century French physiocrat economist, scientist and doctor François Quesnay and his Tableau Economique. Quesnay was a farmer's son and lived at Versailles, where he was King Louis xv's doctor. He believed that French agricultural rents provided the surplus which financed the Court, the French military establishment and the aristocracy's opulent consumption of luxury goods. The difficulty that Quesnay identified was that the surplus from the farmers each year was not enough to feed both the farmers and to pay the taxes that were required to finance the extravagance of the Ancien Regime. As a result, to pay their heavy tax bills farmers ran down their capital assets. This meant that in the future they produced less and found it harder to pay the taxes. As government tax revenue came under pressure, the French government responded by increasing the taxes that had the effect of aggravating a vicious economic cycle, which would only lead to financial collapse. Bacon and Eltis thought in the 1970s that 'Britain's crisis was to a startling extent similar to Quesnay's account of the crisis of the Ancien Régime in France'. The private taxpaying sector was progressively being crowded out by an increasing public sector that had to be paid for by a shrinking private sector.

It is its structural analysis that gives the Bacon-Eltis book its continuing relevance. It is possible to challenge the mechanism by which government spending and borrowing crowds out private investment, whether it is possible to account for the one-for-one employment consequences that the their argument implies, and whether perhaps social security transfer payments played a bigger part in public spending for many years than direct purchases of goods and services, but their central point stands. Public spending has to be paid for through taxation or borrowing which is delayed taxation. That taxation has to be paid for by the private sector and has profound implications for incentives in the private sector and results in losses in output. The result is that as public spending rises beyond a certain point structural rigidities become apparent and manifest themselves in micro-economic markets and in labour markets in particular as well as in a slower rate of growth.

The book played a significant part in stimulating the revival of interest in supply-side matters rooted in the neo-classical framework of economic analysis. This is interesting given that Bacon and Eltis employed the very neo-Keynesian approach that their book challenged and contained little in the way of microeconomic analysis of either the labour market or investment. Moreover, writing in the 1970s the authors probably underestimated the extent to which labour market institutions could be modified and the power of trade unions could be curbed. The Bacon-Eltis thesis continues to be relevant because it sets out what can go wrong when public spending and the tax burden are allowed to rise as a proportion of national income on a sustained basis. In the introduction to the 1996 edition Bacon and Eltis presciently pointed out that the consequences of sustained public spending in terms of rising unemployment, unstable public finances and weak economic growth, even if this process takes place in the context of general macroeconomic stability and low inflation.

Sorry, We Have No Money

Stabilising Britain's public finances

THE THATCHER YEARS stabilised Britain's public finances. Earnings-related social security benefits were cut, although other parts of the social security budget relating to unemployment and invalidity benefit rose. The size and the scope of the state were reduced. The nationalised industries were returned to profit and the government withdrew from directly providing most basic utilities and industries. This programme of denationalisation both helped to reduce the ratio of public expenditure and made the economy more efficient in the medium term as nationalised industries accounted for:

❏ Around 15 per cent of employment;

❏ 20 per cent of capital investment;

❏ And yet only generated some 10 per cent of GDP.

Squeezing public sector pay and capital investment was less successful in the medium term, as were attempts to contain the costs of education and health care. In the second half of the 1980s through to 1992 there were large discretionary increases in public spending.

These issues contributed to the creation of a structural budget deficit that was fully exposed during the recession in the early 1990s when the budget deficit rose to 7 per cent of GDP. The structural deficit was principally caused by increases in public expenditure rather than lower revenue as a result of cuts in marginal tax rate. Nevertheless, Conservative budgets in the 1980s merely remitted some of the fiscal drag that works over time[1] to raise the average tax burden in relation to national income, which did indeed rise during the Conservative period of government.

The combination of a rising tax burden and discretionary

---

1   Fiscal drag is the tendency for the tax burden to rise because the tax system is only partially indexed for inflation, the result being that when the economy is expanding the proportion of national income collected in taxes increases.

restraint on public spending in the early 1980s resulted in a big turnaround in the budget balance, which swung from a deficit of 5 per cent in 1979 to a surplus of 3 per cent in 1989. The position was plainly flattered in the early years by the benefits of oil revenue from the North Sea. At its peak in 1985, output from North Sea oil accounted for close to 6 per cent of GDP. Over two-thirds of it went to the government in corporation tax, petroleum revenue tax or royalties. While in the second half of the 1980s tax revenue was flattered by enhanced tax receipts arising from unsustainable above-trend rates of GDP growth. The public finances also benefited from one-off receipts from the Conservative government's programme of privatisation and asset sales. This transformation of the Public Sector Borrowing Requirement (PSBR) into a Public Sector Debt Repayment between 1986 and 1989 significantly reduced the stock of debt in relation to GDP.

The combination of above-trend economic growth, strong tax receipts and budget surpluses contributed to unrealistic expectations about what was affordable and desirable in terms of public expenditure after 1989. That lack of realism combined with intense political pressure that was accommodated by discretionary increases in almost all areas of programme spending and created a structural budget deficit apparent in the early 1990s. The large surpluses of the 1980s left one beneficial legacy, even if they did contribute to a false sense of optimism. When the British economy entered its next recession in 1990 it did so with a much lower stock of public debt to GDP than during previous slumps. Large deficits of the sort that are incurred in recessions and other adverse shocks could be easily financed given the stock of debt, level of debt interest payments in relation to GDP and the ratio of public expenditure to national income.

The economic focus of the Major administration formed after the 1992 election was largely about rectifying the mistakes of the Prime Minister's period at the Treasury both as Chancellor and Chief Secretary between 1987 and 1990 and those of his

Sorry, We Have No Money

first administration formed after Mrs Thatcher's resignation. The structural budget deficit was eliminated and by 1997 Britain had returned to rough budget balance and was heading for a significant fiscal surplus. This was the result of:

❏ A large discretionary increase in taxation announced in the 1990s;

❏ A sharp fall in price inflation that enabled cash budgets to be cut;

❏ A sustained real squeeze of programme spending that reduced the ratio of public spending to GDP during the 1990s once the economy was again expanding. In addition, the 'Options For Change' Defence White Paper reduced defence spending following the end of the Cold War. An important decision was taken to equalise the national insurance pension age for men and women at 65, that had important implications for containing future unfunded social security liabilities.

In 1997 Britain still had a supply-side problem rooted in public spending

IN 1997 BRITAIN'S PUBLIC FINANCES were stable. Many of the worst structural problems of the late 1960s and 1970s had been overcome. Yet the core structural economic challenge set out in the 1976 White Paper remained. The ratio of public expenditure to GDP was close to 40 per cent. The interaction of the means-tested social security benefits, universal benefits and the national insurance and tax system created acute poverty and unemployment traps. In addition, withdrawing the state from directly producing and financing marketable output and the withdrawal of industrial and regional subsidies, when combined with de-industrialisation exposed an acute regional problem. In UK regions which had been at the heart of the industrial revolution, de-industrialisation was accompanied by a broader de-marketisation. In these regional

Britain's supply-side challenge in the 21st century

economies the public sector and public sector transfer payments crowded out private sector and market-based economic activity by diminishing market incentives.

Some Conservative politicians have described their legacy in 1997 as 'golden':

- ❏ The eighteen years of Conservative government had significantly improved the functioning of the economy.

- ❏ Overdue change in manufacturing was allowed to take place. The subsidised and nationalised sector was largely eliminated.

- ❏ The huge damage done by very high marginal income tax rates that yield little revenue but damage enterprise was ended.

- ❏ The legal framework for industrial relations was significantly modified and the labour market had become much more flexible, yet genuine and significant structural impediments remained.

- ❏ The ratio of public expenditure in relation to national income was still significantly above the optimal level.

- ❏ Although, several decisions had been taken that would reduce the long-term unfunded social security liabilities of the state, an ageing population would mean that long-term health and social security liabilities would become more of a public expenditure burden, in the manner that Nigel Lawson's Green Paper on the future of public expenditure expressed concern about in 1984.

- ❏ In addition, Britain along with other OECD economies would face a new competitive challenge from the emerging economies of Asia led by China and India.

- ❏ The challenge in the 21st century would be to maintain an internationally competitive economy in order to preserve a private sector tax base that could finance the public expenditure and social security transfer payments that would be needed in an ageing society.

A sober assessment of the British economy in 1997 would be that

Conservative ministers had managed to get the British economy back to being a normally performing mature OECD economy. This was largely as a result of bringing inflation down, controlling public spending, privatising its state industries and transforming the labour market. There should have been concern about the structural challenges arising out of a large public sector and the way that these structural rigidities detached many communities and regions from full participation in the labour market and market economy. There should also have been some concern about the extent to which the stabilisation of the UK public finances had been delivered by squeezing public sector capital spending, infrastructure investment and the level and quality of education and training spending. These specific concerns would have been the background to a more general concern about Britain's level of productivity. One of the strengths that would have been identified was the extensive range of private pension provision where pension liabilities were matched by investments and the relatively low level of unfunded public sector pension liabilities compared to other countries. Yet the core supply performance challenge that resulted from a high ratio of public expenditure to national income continued. The issues set out in the 1976 Public Expenditure White Paper remained. It was this high spending ratio that explains why the UK economy appeared not to perform as well as might have been expected given the structural reform of labour market regulation, taxation and the nationalised industries as well as the profound process of disinflation that took place.

New Labour's public expenditure mistake

THE IDEA THAT IN 1997 BRITAIN COULD EASILY AFFORD a massive discretionary increase in public spending, with the sort of room for fiscal adjustment that the editor of the *Financial Times* How To Spend It column could only dream about, was misplaced. Likewise the notion that Britain had underdeveloped public services that if expanded could make rapid inroads into entrenched social problems such as health inequalities, poverty and teenage pregnancy was equally naive. Yet that was the approach that the Labour government took from 1997. Education, health and poverty were to be transformed by increased spending on public services. Having initially reduced their estimate of the trend rate of growth to 2.25 per cent in 1997, Labour Treasury ministers then raised the assumed trend rate of growth. Although they always used a slightly lower estimate when forecasting the public finances, by the end of Labour's period in office the trend rate of growth was estimated to be 2.75 per cent. While national insurance rates were raised and the tax base on companies and savers was extended, the revenue and growth forecasts were disappointing. By 2004 many independent commentators such as the IFS, IMF and OECD were beginning to warn about high levels of public expenditure, a long-term structural budget deficit and an economy that was exposed to risks, because of the level of house prices and household debt.

Sir Nicholas Macpherson, the Permanent Secretary of the Treasury, has summarised the position accurately in his evidence to the Treasury Select Committee, saying that 'a really important point is the one around … the trend rate of growth. There is always a danger that you can delude yourself around the trend rate of growth and I saw that happening in the late 1980s and I have seen it happening again more recently.' (Treasury Select Committee Report June 2010 Budget HC 350.) They were simply too optimistic about the trend rate of growth.

Gordon Brown as Chancellor of the Exchequer did three things that damaged the supply performance of the economy. These were:

- A huge increase in public spending;
- A significant rise in the tax burden;
- A massive extension of means-tested social security transfer programmes that were presented as tax credits.

The increase in spending has aggravated the crowding out effects of public sector spending that were still having a malign impact on

Sorry, We Have No Money

the UK economy in 1997. The higher spending required a higher tax burden that aggravated the problems identified by the 1976 Public Expenditure White Paper and had been partly mitigated by Conservative Budgets. The creation of the tax credits scheme extended the number of households that both pay income tax and receive a means-tested benefit that is withdrawn as income rises. The proportion of households with net rates of withdrawal of over 60 per cent more than doubled. These are the core structural problems that damage the UK economy's supply performance. The high and rising level of public expenditure reallocates national income away from the private sector to the public sector that is the least efficient part of the UK economy, which further aggravates a disappointing productivity performance. Its consequent tax burden, along with the tax credit system the Treasury created, significantly extended the poverty traps in the British tax and benefits system.

The fall in output in the Second Great Contraction

THE SLUMP IN DEMAND that reduced output by over 6 per cent in 2009 exposed the extent of the UK's fiscal problem.

While the tax burden rose sharply after 1997 spending went up faster, creating a structural budget deficit. Private sector output during this slump fell by almost 11 per cent. As tax revenue fell and public expenditure rose to 48 per cent of GDP, the Treasury forecast that the budget deficit would peak at around 12.5 per cent of GDP. The OECD estimated in 2009 that the UK's budget structural or permanent budget deficit was around 10 per cent of GDP. In 2009 the Treasury forecast that it was close to 9 per cent of GDP. These estimates of the structural budget deficit were on the high side; it was probably closer to 7 per cent of GDP. Normally a budget deficit is a second order issue. The decision about the level of borrowing is really a choice about the timing of taxation. When, however, the permanent or structural budget deficit is greater than the realistic trend rate of growth of the economy, the deficit in itself is a source of future public expenditure because the government is building up future debt interest charges at a faster rate than the tax revenue can be expected to expand. In normal circumstances a deficit of around 2.5 per cent of GDP is sustainable; plainly one of 6 or 7 per cent is not in the context of a debt to GDP ratio that was heading for over 80 per cent of GDP. It would be a mistake, however, to assume that once the structural budget deficit is eliminated any chosen level of public expenditure should be accommodated. Experience suggests that even in low inflation environments, high levels of properly tax-financed public expenditure in relation to national income, impedes economic growth.

The British economy's chronic supply-side challenge principally arises out of awkward structural problems created by the level of public expenditure combined with broader regulation of product and labour markets. They are essentially medium and long-term problems, but are now interacting with an immediate and acute fiscal problem that results from the high level of government borrowing and the scale of the structural budget deficit. They relate to the capacity of the British economy to generate high levels of economic welfare for its residents in a sustainable manner. Higher levels of economic welfare means above average levels of GDP per capita compared to the OECD economies, while sustainable means incomes that can be maintained realistically without worries about inflation and an unsustainable balance of payments position in the medium term or an inability to maintain the country's comparative competitive position in the longer term.

This chronic long-term supply-side challenge was fully exposed in the 1970s by a general financial and fiscal crisis. The Callaghan and Thatcher administrations returned Britain to financial stability. The Thatcher and Major governments not only established financial stability but improved the supply performance of the economy. The improvement was often exaggerated. Gordon Brown returned Britain to the kind of public expenditure dynamics that Walter Eltis and Robert Bacon warned about in their structural analysis of the

British economy in the 1970s. That is, an expanding public sector, financed by a contracting private sector that finds it increasing difficult to generate the tax revenue needed to pay for the increasing public sector. The banking crisis has exposed the present unsustainable fiscal position, but it did not create it. Moreover, the resolution of the problems in the financial sector and the structural budget deficit will not resolve Britain's fundamental economic problem of too much public spending and too few producers. This problem will not be touched without fundamental changes in relative prices and incentives. The framework of incentives and relative prices by extension will not be changed without a significant reduction in the proportion of economic activity that is allocated outside of the price mechanism. The part of the economy that is most touched by these cost issues is manufacturing output that is fully exposed to international trade.

Chapter 2: Britain's fiscal problem

THE REALLY IMPORTANT MATTER IN PUBLIC FINANCE is the level of public expenditure.

How a given level of public expenditure is financed is a second order issue. However, some of the methods that a government could choose to finance public spending can be highly damaging to the functioning of a market economy and can create the conditions for dynamic financial instability and inflation. The broad choice is between raising taxes, borrowing and allowing government expenditure to expand the money supply and to create inflation. In modern economic theory and practice, price stability is taken as a necessary condition for an efficient market economy. Modern governments try to avoid creating inflation. A market economy allocates resources using signals about scarcity and efficiency provided by relative prices. If the information yielded by these relative price signals is obscured by a generalised inflation then the cost of extracting information about transactions is increased and the economy operates less efficiently. Price stability and its modern proxy of permanently and reliably low levels of inflation represent a public good in themselves.

Budget deficits represent a choice about the timing of taxation

DELIBERATELY MONETISING PART OF PUBLIC EXPENDITURE to create inflation is not a choice that sensible governments would make. So the choice for finance ministries in financing public expenditure is between taxation and borrowing. That choice is essentially a trade-off about the timing of taxation, given that government debt has to be serviced, the interest and principle paid and repaid out of revenue from taxation. Borrowing to finance a budget deficit today merely raises the future tax burden. A fully funded budget deficit where the gap between spending and taxation is covered by the issuing of bonds sold to the private sector will not result in money creation or inflation, but it will raise future tax liabilities. In normal circumstances finance ministries fully fund their budget deficits by issuing bonds. That avoids an increase in the money supply and inflation being created by governments monetising their deficits, but it does have implications for the level of interest rates and the future tax burden. There are potential complications for the conduct of monetary policy, however, if countries have a large stock of government debt and continuously run large budget deficits even when those deficits are covered by bond issues. These complications are set out in an article entitled 'Some Unpleasant Monetarist Arithmetic' by economists Thomas J. Sargent and Neil Wallace in *Federal Reserve Bank of Minneapolis Quarterly Review 1981.*

Government debt markets yield economic benefits

A PERMANENT BUDGET DEFICIT that is roughly equivalent to an economy's underlying growth rate and the underlying growth in tax revenue does not present much of a problem. In some respects it can have some desirable features. Issuing debt can enable a government to finance its capital investment through borrowing, which means that the benefits and some of the costs of capital spending are shared with future beneficiaries. In addition, many households and financial institutions such as insurance companies find reliable high quality debt instruments, that carry little or no perceived credit risk (and are sometimes called 'risk free') issued by sovereign borrowers, to be convenient investments. And more widely when pricing risk, financial market practitioners find regularly traded, highly liquid 'risk free' government bonds a useful starting point for estimating how to charge for other credit risks. Yield curves derived from government 'risk free' bond markets are used as the benchmark for assessing other credit risks in most advanced economies. The terms 'gilt edged' and 'being in funds' originate from the benefits that 18th century investors discovered from having a plentiful supply of reliable high quality and liquid funds to invest in. There is a significant literature exploring this. It includes P G M Dickson's book 'The Financial Revolution in England: A Study in the Development of Public Credit in England 1689-1756' and Alice Carter's pamphlet 'The English Public Debt in the Eighteenth Century'. In the late 1980s and late 1990s when both the UK and US Treasuries looked as though they were about to run large surpluses for years to come, there were genuine concerns among many institutional investors about the consequences of a lack of supply of new government bonds and an increasingly less liquid government bond market. In the late 1990s these worries were sufficiently serious that President Clinton's Council of Economic Advisers offered a summary analysis of the issues in the annual *Economic Report of the President*.

The problem with a large structural budget deficit

IT IS MISLEADING TO THINK that a permanent or structural budget deficit in excess of an economy's underlying economic rate of growth or more importantly its growth of tax revenue within its chosen tax structure can be ignored. First, a borrowing requirement in excess of the growth in tax revenue means that a government is accumulating debt at a faster rate than its revenue from taxes. It is increasing public expenditure through higher debt service costs at a faster rate than it will receive additional tax revenue. Second, government borrowing is not costless. It implies future taxation and potentially borrowing can raise interest rates and crowd out private sector borrowing and investment.

Government deficits and interest rates

THE EXTENT TO WHICH A GOVERNMENT borrowing money in the capital markets will influence interest rates will depend on how open its capital markets are and how integrated they are in practice into world capital markets; how much competition there is from other borrowers, which largely turns on where in the economic cycle the economy is. In a closed economy with capital markets closed to the international markets, government borrowing inter alia is likely to have a powerful and direct effect on interest rates, because of its size. In open capital markets an individual government borrowing programme has to be very large indeed to exert an influence. The US Treasury is a sufficiently large borrower to have that sort of influence and its level of borrowing does appear to influence interest rates and it does appear to have the capacity to crowd out private sector borrowing by raising the real cost of borrowing. In normal circumstances increased government borrowing by an individual government to fund a sustainable budget deficit may have little impact on interest rates in open capital markets. Where a government is borrowing to fund an unsustainably high deficit and the markets become concerned about inflation, default risk and future interest rate risks, such a government will have to pay a premium to sell its bonds. Governments that continue to borrow in those circumstances will have to pay a higher interest rate to sell their debt and that will increase borrowing costs for the private sector and will have implications for future capital accumulation and long-term economic growth.

The 1929 public works White Paper and Treasury orthodoxy in the 1920s

IN A DEEP SLUMP IN OUTPUT there is a tension in fiscal policy between active discretionary stimulus measures and the need to ensure that budget deficits resulting from the fall in output do not put up interest rates that crowd out private borrowing, preventing a natural recovery from taking place. In Britain this debate remains coloured by the arguments that surrounded economic policy in the 1920s and 1930s. The classic statement of this concern was set out in the British Treasury's White Paper on public works published in 1929. John Maynard Keynes had published a paper for the British Liberal Party arguing that unemployment could be reduced if idle balances of companies that were being held in the money markets were mobilised by the government borrowing them to spend on public works programmes to reduce unemployment. The Treasury responded by arguing that the increased government borrowing would result in higher interest rates and those higher interest rates would mean less private sector investment. The result would be that at best government spending replaced private spending.

This famous White Paper has to be looked at, however, in its particular historical context. The Treasury paper was part of a series of memoranda put together by Whitehall departments to rebut the suggestions for public works programmes being made by David Lloyd George and Keynes. The Treasury memorandum was just one of these memoranda. It has gone down in economic history as the locus classicus of the orthodox Treasury opinion that deficit spending even in a slump simply crowds out private sector activity and investment through higher interest rates. Modern historiography (for example Peter Clarke, 'Churchill's Economic Ideas, 1900-1930') suggests that this series of separate departmental memoranda may not have been principally commissioned to rebut Lloyd George's pamphlet 'We can Conquer Unemployment', but rather to answer the concerns of some Conservative cabinet ministers. These included the Home Secretary, Sir William Joynson Hicks, and the Minister of Labour, Sir Arthur Steel Maitland, who were becoming attracted to ideas of Keynes and Lloyd George and put forward a scheme for public works. This may explain why the White Paper, far from being a magisterial statement of Treasury argument, is a hodge-podge of different papers hurriedly put together to address different parts of Lloyd George's proposals as they affected different government departments. The Treasury's memorandum was based on Churchill's adaptation of an article in *Economica* written by Treasury official R Hawtrey in 1925. This argued on theoretical

Britain's fiscal problem

grounds that unless there was an inflationary expansion of credit, government borrowing could not increase employment.

An important feature of the debate about using active fiscal policy to stimulate demand during a slump and the 1929 White Paper, is its economic context. The British economy in the 1920s suffered from an uncompetitive exchange rate that could not be modified because of the decision to return to the Gold Standard at its pre-First World War rate of exchange, the effects of which were explained in Keynes's famous pamphlet 'The Economic Consequences of Mr Churchill'. The chosen exchange rate was $4.86. In effect Britain had informally returned to that exchange rate as early as 1918 and it meant that against the dollar sterling was about 10 per cent overvalued and was even more over valued against some European currencies such as the French franc. Once Britain was formally on the gold standard maintaining the exchange rate was difficult because France with a competitive exchange rate experienced a strong demand for her exports that was matched by an inflow of gold which aggravated the British problem.

The Poincaré stabilisation of the 1920s and French fiscal crowding in

IN THE SECOND HALF OF THE 1920S France was enjoying the fruits of the Poincaré fiscal stabilisation. Kenneth Mouré explored French policy that contrasted sharply with that of Britain in both the 1920s and 1930s in 'Managing the Franc Poincaré Economic Understanding and Political Constraint in Monetary Policy 1928-36' (1991). In the early 1920s France experienced an intense financial crisis and very high rates of inflation. In 1926, after the collapse of the Cartel des Gauches, Poincaré became Prime Minister and Finance Minister and introduced a series of stabilisation measures. France returned to the Gold Standard in 1928 at a rate one-fifth lower than the pre-war rate and government deficits that had been the source of the previous inflation as a result of monetisation were eliminated. In the second half of the 1920s inflation, nominal and real interest rates fell sharply. The combination of a competitively valued exchange rate, the repayment and avoidance of deficits created the conditions not only for export growth, but positive crowding in effects and increased domestic investment as a result of the tight fiscal policy in the context of looser monetary conditions arising from a realistic exchange rate. At the time this was regarded as something of an economic miracle. French experience in the 1920s illustrates the way that necessary yet potentially painful macroeconomic stabilisation measures can yield swift benefits.

In the 1920s the British economy performed badly, because its manufacturing sector was made uncompetitive as a result of a high exchange rate. Feinstein, Temin and Toniolo show in 'The World Economy between the Wars' (2008) that inappropriate monetary policy aggravated real problems that would have been very difficult to manage in any circumstances. These were dislocations in trade that arose as result of the First World War, where Britain lost historic pre-war export markets. To this burden an artificially overvalued exchange rate was added.

Arguably in the context of a very tight domestic monetary policy that could not be modified because of the need to maintain foreign confidence in sterling, a significant fiscal stimulus may have increased domestic interest rates and it would not have addressed the central defect in policy. Higher interest rates in 1929 would not have simply risked damage to private sector investment, but would have increased the government's own debt service charge, given that around one-third was so-called floating debt that had to be regularly refinanced and higher interest rates would have increased that element of public expenditure. The core problem was a flawed monetary policy regime. What was needed was a completely different monetary policy and a competitive exchange rate. The Treasury memorandum on finance points out that Lloyd George's pamphlet was fully committed to the government's monetary policy

Britain's fiscal problem

and quotes from it: that 'inflation, whilst it would temporarily solve our problem, would mean the departure from the gold standard, a reduction in the real standard of life of those at present employed and the grave risk of economic collapse in the long run. It can be entirely ruled out'. What the Treasury paper did not have was a serious estimate of the multiplier effect that increased government spending might have had. Although in fairness to its authors in 1929 the multiplier had yet to be fully worked up as an economic concept by Joan Robinson and Lord Khan.

When Britain abandoned the Gold Standard in 1931 and was able to run an appropriately loose domestic monetary policy combined with a much more competitive exchange rate, the British economy performed well relative to that of other major economies, without using discretionary fiscal policies. The reason for this was that Britain had a distinctive economic history in the inter-war years. It amounted to a deliberate domestic deflation to return the price level to its pre-1914 level in order to reconstruct the pre-war Gold Standard. This led to a protracted domestic UK slump in demand and output. The result was that in the 1920s Britain missed out on the international boom that was particularly apparent in the US in the second half of the 1920s and commemorated in the literary fiction of 'The Great Gatsby'. In the 1930s output fell less than in other economies, stabilised earlier and recovered relatively well. In contrast the French economy, although initially weathering well the early part of the economic crisis compared to other countries at least until 1931, did not perform as well as the British economy in the 1930s. Part of the reason was that France stuck to the Gold Standard. France was on gold until the Popular Front government was forced off it in 1936. This is apparently explained because French policy makers were politically constrained by the fear that loosening monetary policy risked returning to the inflation and financial instability of the early 1920s. It is probably a mistake to read too much into Churchill's statement of Treasury orthodoxy in 1929. It was a political document worked up to deal with internal

Sorry, We Have No Money

critics inside the Cabinet. Moreover, it has to be considered in the particular circumstances of the time and the particular monetary policy and exchange rate regime that was in place.

When the euro-zone was being created twenty years ago following the Delors Report on European Monetary Union in 1989, its protagonists sometimes likened it to a modern day gold standard. Although it was misleading in that the euro is just another paper or fiat currency[1], its consequences for individual countries involved were likely to be similar to those of Britain in the 1920s. Portugal, Ireland, Greece and Spain have recently been faced with financial and economic constraints arising out of an inappropriate monetary policy and an uncompetitive international exchange rate analogous to those of Britain in the 1920s.

In an economy that has capital markets in practice integrated into the international economy, where monetary policy can address domestic circumstances and the exchange rate is flexible, fiscal policy probably can stimulate demand. And that stimulus will not necessarily result in an increase in domestic interest rates that will vitiate the public sector's actions. There will be leakages through increased imports, so that it is more difficult for smaller open economies to make successful use of such fiscal policy. The higher the stock of the initial level of government debt and the greater the perceived extent of the permanent or structural budget deficit, the greater the risk that interest rates will rise not so much through crowding out, but concerns about the real creditworthiness of the government as a borrower in terms of default or its willingness to tolerate higher inflation. Governments that face adverse economic shocks are able to use fiscal policy to manage the adjustment provided they have reasonable levels of debt in relation to GDP and control

---

1   A fiat currency is one that has been declared by a government to be legal tender, despite the fact that it has no intrinsic value and is not backed by reserves. Historically, most currencies were based on physical commodities such as gold or silver, but fiat money is based solely on the issuing authority's guarantee to pay the stated (face) amount on demand.

Britain's fiscal problem

over their own monetary policy and exchange rate. In recent years policy makers have been too ready to dismiss completely the potential use of fiscal policy as part of demand management. Having acknowledged that, it is also worth remembering what Poincaré achieved in France, where he combined a competitive exchange rate with a tight fiscal policy that resulted in a crowding in of private investment.

Government debt imposes a real economic cost: the chimera of burdenless debt

EVEN IF GOVERNMENT BORROWING does not determine the level of interest rates by the extent of its borrowing, its debt will have to be financed through taxation. That results in tax payers in general having to make transfer payments to bond-owning rentiers. Rentiers tend to be either wealthier households or institutions investing on their behalf, so government debt service payments represent a payment to richer households. In an economy integrated into world capital and money markets a proportion of the debt will be owed to foreign bond holders, so payments on it represents a transfer of resources from one country's taxpayers to the residents of another. These represent genuine transfers of income wealth and economic welfare. For many years following the end of the Second World War in 1945, Keynesian economists believed that government debt imposed no burden on an economy and that it was costless. This was largely as result of an important article written by a British economist, Abba Lerner, who was educated in a rabbinical school which he left at sixteen and started a career as a tailor in the East End of London, before going on to become one of the most influential socialist economists in the 20th century. Lerner developed a distinctive theory of functional finance in which the job of the government borrowing requirement was to ensure that there was always sufficient demand in the economy to ensure full employment. His

Sorry, We Have No Money

arresting point was that government debt service was essentially a transfer from one set of citizens to another, so that overall the economic welfare of the citizens was unaltered. This clever argument to justify the regular use of budget deficits ignored the incentive and deadweight effects that the necessary tax burden would impose on the economy. Lerner took no account of the consequences of such transfers when the economy was operating in open capital markets. Lerner's assertion that government debt carried no cost or overall burden resulted in the notion of burdenless debt. This was not just a recondite or academic discussion. The concept influenced many economists and policy makers, and it certainly influenced the British Treasury for many years, despite the fact that it was plainly wrong.

Borrowing heavily in wartime and other emergencies is not a problem

PERIODIC BUDGET DEFICITS that reflect the state of the economic cycle or realistically affordable borrowing to finance rigorously costed capital investment that will generate benefits in excess of its costs do not represent a problem. A large structural or permanent deficit that is increasing the stock of government debt and the costs of debt service charges within public expenditure at a faster rate than tax revenue is, however, a problem. Traditionally governments have borrowed huge amounts in emergencies. In the past these emergencies have been principally associated with war. The British national debt was accumulated throughout the 18th century as a consequence of the wars with Bourbon France and then peaked in the Napoleonic Wars. After 1815 in the long period of peace with few major wars the national debt declined in relation to national income, but dramatically rose again during the First and Second World Wars in the 20th century. In the modern context very high levels of borrowing would be acceptable not just to finance war, but to deal with other economic and social shocks. These would include a huge loss of output of the sort that European economies have experienced between 2008 and 2009. It would also include borrowing to deal with other shocks that might arise from a major health epidemic or the impact of natural disaster such as a tsunami or an earthquake. It is helpful if the stock of government debt is relatively low at the start of such a crisis because the significant increase in the level of debt as a result of the crisis is then affordable. This means that in periods of peacetime expansion deficits need to be contained and where the stock of government debt is high in relation to GDP it needs to be reduced over time. Running large deficits during an unusual and temporary, economic or environmental shock may not be a problem, but running large deficits in peacetime or during periods of steady economic expansion do create public expenditure and taxation problems.

Should governments deliberately tolerate inflation to liquidate public debts?

IN POST-WAR BRITAIN inflation played a significant part in reducing the real burden of government debt incurred during the First and Second World Wars. In 1950 public debt represented 275 per cent of national income. By the mid 1970s it had fallen to 52 per cent of GDP as a result of GDP and prices increasing. Between 1975 and 1979 it fell from 53.8 per cent to 43.9 per cent of GDP. That 10 percentage point fall took place at a time when the annual average deficit was close to 6 per cent of GDP and real GDP growth was sluggish. What reduced the size of the debt in relation to money GDP was inflation. There are some commentators who have suggested that higher inflation is a reasonable price to pay to reduce the real value of government debt, and indeed business leaders are tempted to advocate inflation. This temptation should be resisted, not least because in the UK 19 per cent of the government's outstanding debt is index linked. So that inflation would not be as easy an option as it once was.

The main reason why governments should not resort to inflation is that in a market economy based on price signals it distorts information and raises transaction costs. Shortly after the Bank of England was made operationally independent and charged with meeting an inflation target set by the government, economists in its Monetary Analysis Division examined the benefits of price stability in an article in the *Bank of England Quarterly Bulletin*, 'Quantifying some benefits of price stability' (August 1997). They found that because inflation distorts the demand for money and aggravates the distortion created by taxationbecause the tax system is only partially indexed for inflation, it imposes identifiable costs on the economy. Lowering inflation by 2 percentage points could generate an additional 0.2 per cent of GDP per year. There is no reason to believe that this position has changed.

The IMF considered the role that inflation could now play in reducing the real value of public debt in a policy paper 'Strategies for Fiscal Consolidation in the Post-Crisis World' in 2010. There is still scope for so-called seignorage, but the IMF judges that it is more limited than it was in G7 economies because the level of 'the money base' is relatively lower than it once was. While an unexpected rise in the rate of inflation would reduce the value of existing debts, long-term interest rates would probably rise with inflation, so that any maturing debt would have to be refinanced at higher rates. The IMF warns that any gain from inflation has to be set against the huge distortions in resource allocation the inflation creates. These reduce economic growth and once inflation is in play it is difficult to keep it under control and there are substantial output costs involved in bring inflation back down again. The UK's experience of losing control over inflation at the end of the 1980s, and the consequences of the policies that were needed to bring it back under control in the early 1990s illustrate the IMF's point well. Low and stable inflation of around 2 per cent is a genuine benefit

Britain's fiscal problem

that should not be given up or compromised. There is an argument about what the UK's inflation target should be and economists at the IMF have wondered whether the UK should raise it to 4 per cent. In my judgment relaxing the present target, which has already been relaxed compared to the less 2.5 per cent RPI (excluding mortgage interest rates) that was in place in 1997, would be a mistake. What is clear is that a deliberate return to double-digit inflation would be a serious policy error.

Britain has a budget deficit problem

BRITAIN WENT INTO TO THE CREDIT CRUNCH in 2007 with its public finances in an awkward condition. Leaving aside the medium and long-term structural problems that arise out of the ratio of government spending to GDP, it already had a significant structural deficit. Britain's budget arithmetic was based on over-optimistic assumptions about:

❏ The size of the economy;

❏ The trend rate of growth;

❏ The potential growth of tax revenue.

It was plain for some four or five years before the credit crunch that public expenditure was rising rapidly within GDP. Tax revenue had not been increasing at the rate that the Treasury was expecting. The result was the creation of structural or permanent budget deficit that was beyond the rough 2.5 per cent to 2.75 per cent of GDP level that was realistic and a stock of government debt that was rising faster than the underlying growth in the tax base. Moreover, it was evident that there was a significant bubble element in the UK economy given the performance of the housing market. At the start of 2007 the economy was plainly overheating and operating beyond its capacity as it had done for several years, yet at the peak of the cycle after many years of economic expansion there was a significant and rising budget deficit, which implied a large structural budget deficit.

In 2007 when the credit crunch hit, the UK's public finances were less well placed to deal with a major adverse economic shock than they were in the early 1990s. The UK entered a major slump in output with a significantly higher stock of public debt to GDP. In 1990 the ratio was 27 per cent, in 2007 it was over 36 per cent. Moreover, debts incurred in the context of low levels of inflation or even potential deflation are much harder to manage than debts where their real burden is eroded by increases in the price level. Part of the explanation for the fall in the UK's public debt to GDP ratio in the 1970s and early 1980s was rapid price inflation.

The problem that the UK faces is not so much the scale of the bank bailout or the very large budget deficit created by the slump in output and the discretionary measures taken to mitigate it. The problem is a very large permanent budget deficit that will remain once output recovers and the economy is expanding. In December 2009 the Treasury in the pre-Budget report forecast that the Budget deficit for 2009-10 would be £177.6 billion, or 12.6 per cent of GDP. In five years' time the Treasury was projecting a deficit of 4.4 per cent of GDP, which would have been much higher than any realistic assessment of sustainable budget deficit. Moreover, that projection was based on highly optimistic assumptions. These included a rapid return to the trend rate of growth of around 2.5 percent followed by four years of significantly above-trend growth in GDP of 3.25 per cent. And despite three or four years of rapid economic growth the Treasury still estimated that there will be spare capacity in the economy. After a period of four years of GDP expansion at over 3 per cent the budget deficit would still have been 4.4 per cent of GDP. That meant that the structural budget deficit must be much higher. Estimating GDP growth and tax revenue and expenditure is always difficult, but a more realistic estimate of the structural budget deficit was probably 6 to 7 per cent of GDP.

Britain's fiscal problem

The Coalition government's necessary emergency budget in June 2010

IN 2007 AFTER A PERIOD of unsustainable profits, financial services pay and bonuses and a prolonged boom in property prices, tax receipts were artificially high. Public spending increased from 41 per cent of GDP in 2006-07 to 48 per cent in 2009-10. As output fell by over 6 per cent taxes fell by two percentage points of GDP, creating an unsustainable budget deficit. As the Treasury Budget Redbook in June 2010 points out, tax receipts in the UK have averaged around 38 per cent of GDP over the last twenty years and have never exceeded 40 per cent of national income. From 2002 onwards tax receipts, actually collected, came in consistently below the Treasury's Redbook projections. The 2003 Redbook projected that total receipts would rise steadily from 37.6 per cent of GDP in 2002-03 to 40.1 per cent in 2006-07. The tax collected was consistently 1.3 to 2 percentage points of GDP lower. In 2002-03 the proportion of GDP collected in tax was 36.3 per cent and in 2006-07 it was 38.6 per cent.

The UK's fiscal challenge is summarised in the Coalition government's June 2010 Emergency Budget Redbook. The IMF Fiscal Monitor in May 2010 forecast that the UK would have the highest public borrowing requirement in the G20. It also estimated that the UK's structural deficit was the highest among all the OECD countries. The IMF Fiscal Monitor confirmed what the OECD had said about the UK public finances in the OECD Economic Outlook No 87 in May 2010 and what the European Commission said in its Spring Forecast in May 2010.

The Coalition has announced audacious measures to stabilise the public finances. George Osborne's approach is firmly rooted in the international fiscal consolidation literature, which suggests that public finances are most effectively stabilised when public spending is cut rather than trying to maintain spending and using taxes to eliminate the deficit. OECD and IMF research suggests that public

Sorry, We Have No Money

sector capital investment should be protected, taxes on capital and labour should be minimised, and the social security benefits should be reformed to reduce their malign effect on employment incentives. Ideally, 80 per cent of the adjustment should come about through lower spending and not more than 20 per cent through higher taxes. Overall the Emergency Budget and the measures announced by Alistair Darling in the last Labour Budget in March 2010 will put up taxes and reduce spending by £128 billion between 2010-11 and 2015-16. Of this, 77 per cent of the fiscal tightening is planned to be delivered through lower spending amounting to £99 billion and net increase in taxes of £28 billion. These measures are projected progressively to reduce borrowing from 11 per cent of GDP in 2009-10 to 1.1 per cent in 2015-16. The rise in the stock of public debt in relation to GDP will start to stabilise, peaking at 70.3 per of GDP in 2013-14 and will then begin to fall. Public expenditure is projected to fall from 47.5 per cent of GDP in 2010-10 to 39.8 per cent of GDP in 2015-16.

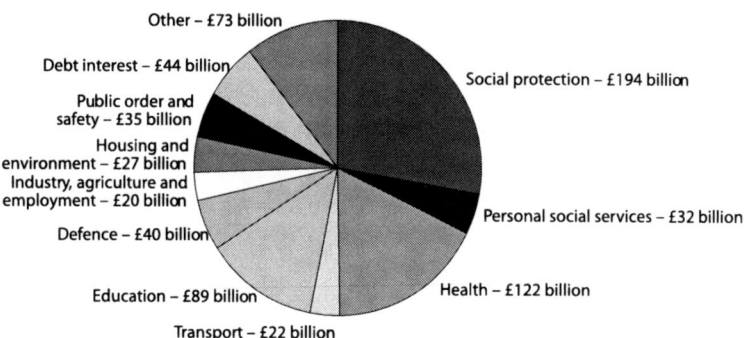

FIGURE 2.1: *Government spending 2010-11 (Source: HM Treasury 2010 near-cash projections)*

Britain's fiscal problem

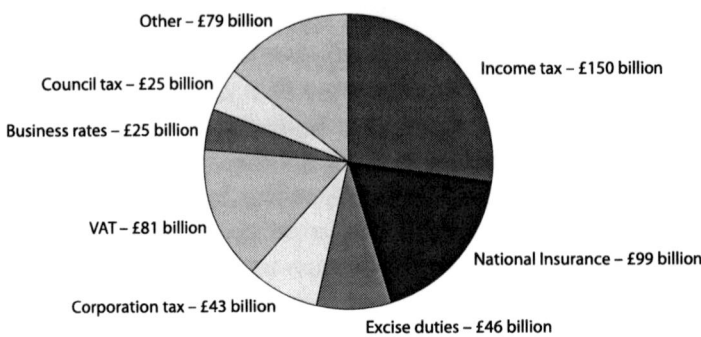

Total receipts: £548 billion

Other – £79 billion

Income tax – £150 billion

Council tax – £25 billion

Business rates – £25 billion

VAT – £81 billion

National Insurance – £99 billion

Corporation tax – £43 billion

Excise duties – £46 billion

FIGURE 2.2: *Government receipts 2010-11 (Source: OBR, 2010-11 estimates)*

The government's plans are a realistic approach that addresses the borrowing challenges that the IMF and other organisations identified. There are arguments to be had about the precise timing of the increases in taxes and the projected reductions in public spending. The taxes go up in the early years and the spending mainly comes down in the later years. There is always a danger that the spending adjustments do not come through in full. Given the scale of the UK's fiscal problem and that output appeared to stabilise at the end of 2009, the Coalition government is right to make a swift start on this necessary adjustment to stabilise the public finance, even though there are risks that in its early stages, the normal multiplier effects may weaken GDP growth.

In the 1970s the deficit peaked at 9 per cent of GDP. The real value of the stock of debt was eroded by inflation and Britain's public finances were about to enjoy the benefits of North Sea oil. As a proportion of output, oil production peaked in the mid-1980s at around 6 per cent of GDP. About 70 per cent of these oil revenues accrued to the Treasury as royalties, corporation tax or petroleum revenue tax. The UK public finances will not be helped by that source of revenue now. In addition, in the 1970s and 1980

Sorry, We Have No Money

the British government owned important basic industries whose finances could be rectified reducing the budget deficit and could then be privatised, giving the Treasury huge one-off sources of revenue that could be used to repay debt. These were very significant assets that accounted for around 10 per cent of GDP in 1979. There are no similar assets available for sale to keep the stock of debt in check. Today Britain has neither an obvious new source of revenue such as that from North Sea oil nor nationalised industries to sell, or even broadband frequencies to auction off as was done in the 1990s. The present budget deficits are therefore going to be more difficult to manage than the budget deficits in the 1970s. Today they appear larger and there are no obvious new sources of revenue or potential windfalls available from the sale of state assets.

Cutting the UK's structural budget deficit to a realistically affordable level is a necessary condition for financial stability in the medium term. Given the range of political, economic and environmental shocks that could affect the country, part of that realism should include reducing the stock of public debt over time so that the government can readily borrow in a crisis. This means in practice running surpluses in a regular and consistent manner when the economy is operating close to full capacity during the more mature phases of economic expansion.

Eliminating the budget deficit will not be sufficient for an optimal economic performance

SIMPLY ELIMINATING THE UK'S STRUCTURAL BUDGET DEFICIT and reducing the stock of government debt over the medium term may be a necessary condition for financial stability, but it will not on its own ensure that the economy will generate the maximum amount of economic welfare for its residents. Tackling the budget deficit is simply about sorting out the immediate issues of financial stability. The revised spending plans will bring the ratio of public spending to GDP down to 39.8 per cent that will leave it significantly above the 35 per cent level, where it achieves little at the margin in improved social and economic results and imposes costs that slow economic growth and welfare. The real challenge for policy makers is to address the long-term structural impediments that hinder the British economy from operating in an optimal way. The heart of those structural impediments are the level of public expenditure, its productivity and the malign consequences of the deadweight costs of the taxation necessary to finance it. The need to address these structural impediments is compounded by the competitive challenge that is presented by the emerging economies and China and India in particular.

Sorry, We Have No Money

Chapter 3: How effective is fiscal policy in demand management terms?

ACTIVE USE OF fiscal policy as part of demand management was generally accepted as the appropriate method of ensuring that resources were fully employed and demand was maintained or contracted as needed over the economic cycle until the 1970s. The role of fiscal policy in active demand management was central to the Keynesian revolution of the 1940s.

Its use was discredited as part of the collapse of the Keynesian system in the 1970s. Fiscal policy was until recently perceived as at best weak and ineffective and at worst distorting and potentially destabilising. There were four main reasons why policy makers became sceptical about the use of fiscal policy as part of demand management. These were:

❏ Its empirical record of effectiveness;

❏ The practical difficulties of timing policy implementation;

❏ The long-term consequences for the structure of microeconomic decisions; and,

❏ Highly theoretical concerns about so-called neo-Ricardian equivalence that suggested policy would not work to stabilise the economic cycle even if policy makers wanted to use it.

The discrediting of the fiscal policy as a tool of economic management took place in the US in the late 1960s. The combination of the cost of the Vietnam War and Lyndon Johnson's Great Society programmes resulted in inflation and pressures on the American balance of payments. The American economy needed to slow down. The Johnson administration tried to deal with this by raising taxes, which had no impact. American economic activity did not slow until the Federal Reserve Board tightened monetary conditions and raised interest rates. In Britain the seminal event was the 1981 Budget. Sir Geoffrey Howe tightened fiscal policy in order to reduce a structural budget deficit in the trough of a slump in output – the spring of 1981. Many economists said that this action was pro-cyclical rather than counter-cyclical and would vitiate a recovery in output. As things turned out GDP started to rise and the economy then steadily expanded for some seven or eight years.

How effective is fiscal policy in demand management terms?

At the same time the exchange rate fell, domestic interest rates were lowered and the economy in the early 1980s was further stimulated by a real balances or 'Pigou effect' arising from a greater than expected fall in inflation boosting the real value of money balances held by households and firms. This appeared to confirm the importance of monetary conditions compared to discretionary changes in taxation and spending that only directly affected a small ratio of total output, although the multiplier effects are always greater than the simple cash numbers may suggest.

Discretionary changes in taxation and spending as part of macro-economic demand management were increasingly perceived as a source of instability. By the time they took effect the economy had moved on rather than kicking in when needed as changes in taxes and spending amplified the economic cycle. Milton Friedman's charge against fiscal policy was that it was pro-cyclical rather than counter-cyclical. Also, the level and composition of public expenditure, the tax burden and marginal tax rates were increasingly seen as important in shaping the evolution of the economy's supply performance in the medium term.

Not only did discretionary changes in taxation and spending amplify rather than smooth the cycle, they had malign structural effects on the economy. Increased government spending and new public sector programmes were politically difficult to cut once the immediate macroeconomic rationale for their introduction was over. Frequent changes in tax rates and the structure of income, corporation and capital taxes distort economic decision making and undermines the long-term supply performance of the economy.

If this catalogue of defects was not enough to finish off the appetite of policy makers for fiscal policy, then the theoretical work done by Robert Barro in the 1970s did. Barro, who as mentioned earlier has also done a lot of work on new growth theory and how economies experience and respond to adverse economic shocks, explored some concerns about the consequences of government debt that were first raised by the British economist David Ricardo

Sorry, We Have No Money

in the 19th century. The essence of Barro's work is that people try and smooth their consumption to match some idea of their permanent income and they have a long-term interest in the welfare of future generations. A government that tries to spend its way out of recession by spending money and running government deficits will find that its efforts are vitiated by the offsetting behaviour of private sector households. They will recognise that one way or another government deficits will have to be paid for by future increases in taxation and therefore cut their spending and increase their savings to pay for the future increased tax burden. While this idea of 'neo-Ricardian equivalence' may seem very academic and remote, its influence on the thinking of policy makers, particularly central bank and finance ministry officials, should not be underestimated. The OECD Economic Outlook in May 2010, for example, suggests that about 40 per cent of any fiscal stimulus financed by government borrowing is offset by the private sector raising its saving in the short term to meet the expected rise in the future tax burden. The OECD estimate is based on its economists' own calculations, which are consistent with other recent studies that suggest offsetting effects ranging between 10 and 50 per cent.

Having been comprehensively dismissed for a generation, fiscal policy has certainly been back in a spectacular fashion since the autumn of 2008. It reflects the scale of the problems central banks face that so many governments have turned to fiscal measures. Many of the world's central bankers now accept it as well. They include Chairman of the Federal Reserve Board and most of the regional federal reserve bank presidents, as well as the Governor of the Bank of England, Mervyn King, who had previously expressed reservations about the discretionary fiscal policy on the basis of concern about neo-Ricardian effects.

In many respects the IMF led the world down this road. It changed in its own attitude to fiscal policy and the speed of that change can be seen from its publications in autumn 2008. In November 2008 it published a supplement to its *World Economic Outlook*. The previous

How effective is fiscal policy in demand management terms?

month the core judgment in chapter 1, 'Policy Challenges For The Global Economy', the IMF's advice on the role of fiscal policy was cautious and hedged. The US fiscal stimulus in February 2008 was judged to be well timed, but regarding the:

'potential costs of these measures (the TARP and housing bailout measures) and the need for medium-term consolidation, however, adjustment measures will be required elsewhere.'

Likewise in relation to the euro-zone:

'fiscal policy is already providing support to the euro area economy through automatic stabilisers and discretionary measures in some countries' and the *'limited scope for further fiscal easing available under the revised Stability and Growth Pact should be used to focus public resources on stabilising financial conditions, as needed.'*

Within a month, in the November edition of the *World Economic Outlook: Update,* the tone had changed decisively. The IMF position was now that the:

'room for further easing of (monetary) policy is limited as policy rates are already close to the zero bound. These are conditions where broad based fiscal stimulus is likely to be warranted. Fiscal stimulus can be effective if it is well targeted, supported by accommodative monetary policy, and implemented in counties that have fiscal space.'

The interesting thing is that before the financial crisis that emerged in 2007, attitudes to fiscal policy among US economists were already changing. This change in attitude reflected new evidence about the impact of the Bush tax cuts in 2001. Most economists, including those who supported cuts in marginal rates for supply-side reasons, assumed that the story would be much like the Ford administration's fiscal stimulus in 1975, when tax refunds were received by taxpayers after output had already started to recover. Empirical work assessing the impact of the 2001 tax cuts suggested that they had a positive impact at an appropriate stage of the economic cycle. As a result the balance of mainstream economic thinking about the efficacy of fiscal policy had began to shift, before the financial crisis fully took hold.

Sorry, We Have No Money

A group of economists reported their work on the effects of the Bush tax cut in the *American Economic Review* in December 2006 (vol. 96 No5) in an article entitled 'Household Expenditure and Income Tax Rebates of 2001'. They found that households spent much of their income tax rebate. Between 20 and 40 per cent of the rebates were spent in the three months following receipt of the cheque from the Internal Revenue Service. Overall, two-thirds of the rebates were spent within three months. In national accounts terms the tax rebates provided a substantial stimulus to the national economy in 2001. They added $38 billion (about 2.2 per cent) to personal consumption expenditure and 7.5 per cent to non-durable expenditure in the third quarter of 2001. The behaviour of the savings ratio, which fell from 1.9 per cent in the first quarter of 2001 to 1.2 per cent in the second quarter, before recovering to 3.4 per cent in the fourth quarter, was also consistent with evidence of the fiscal stimulus having 'anticipatory' effects. It appears that consumers ran down their savings and maintained or brought forward their consumption in the knowledge that the tax rebates would be coming.

This article is significant in modifying economists' views about the efficacy of fiscal policy in macroeconomic management. Dollar for dollar it was able to track consumer spending being raised as a result of the tax cut and changes in consumer behaviour consistent with consumers being forward looking. It may appear dull and technical, but it represents a significant counter-factual to most of the evidence accumulated over the previous forty or more years. There is no point in pretending that for policy makers and economists, who had come to accept Milton Friedman's judgment about the weakness of fiscal policy, this piece of work is a challenge they cannot ignore. So, however well used an economist or policy maker may be to notions of the clumsiness and tardiness of fiscal policy or influenced by concepts of neo-Ricardian equivalence, the arguments surrounding fiscal policy as a potential stimulus need to be re-examined.

It would be mistaken to regard this renewed interest in active

How effective is fiscal policy in demand management terms?

counter-cycle fiscal policy simply as either a political response or some kind of New Keynesian intellectual agenda. Among the economists looking afresh at these issues over the last year are Martin Feldstein and Michael Boskin. They are former Chairs of the Council of Economic Advisers in the Reagan and Bush administrations and are main stream neo-classical economists of a politically conservative cast of mind. Martin Feldstein has proposed that a fiscal stimulus should automatically kick in if certain criteria about output or employment are triggered.

In July 2008 the Federal Reserve Bank of San Francisco organised a seminar to look at the research on the effects of fiscal stimulus as a policy tool. Michael Boskin led the discussion and noted that there was now a consensus among American economists that counter-cyclical fiscal policy could mitigate the damage of economic slowdowns. Boskin pointed to two changes of judgment about the efficacy of fiscal policy. The first is the wide recognition that there is little evidence to suggest that consumers actually modify their behaviour in response to government deficits. That disposes of the theoretical concern about neo-Ricardian equivalence. The second change is the recognition that in some circumstances fiscal policy may work faster and more directly than changes in monetary conditions that normally act with a variable lag of between six and eighteen months.

There was in 2008 a growing consensus that discretionary fiscal policies could usefully stimulate economic activity in certain circumstances. Ideally such policies should meet the criteria of the three Ts: they should be timely, targeted and temporary. The key thing was that they should give a temporary boost to demand, but not become entrenched in a manner that permanently increases the stock of public debt, crowding out private sector activity and capital investment in the medium term. After the collapse of Lehman Brothers and elimination of conventional monetary policy as an effective and independent instrument of policy in September 2008

Sorry, We Have No Money

economists and governments turned to discretionary fiscal policy as the only practical tool available to stabilise the fall in output.

In those extraordinary circumstances in the autumn of 2008 analogous to the circumstances that Keynes had written about so vividly in the 'General Theory of Employment, Interest and Money' in 1936, I too supported discretionary fiscal policies. It appeared that monetary policy only existed to the extent that fiscal policy backed the banking system; interest rates were at a level where changing them would no longer influence economic behaviour and output was collapsing. In BBC radio interviews in November 2008 I advocated a fiscal stimulus to try to stabilise a fall of output in the British economy of around 5 or 6 per cent of GDP. The slump turned out to be if anything worse than that. From peak to trough GDP fell by 6.4 per cent and the fall in private sector output was closer to 11 per cent.

Internationally, from October 2008 fiscal policy staged a dramatic comeback. Among the countries that announced, or in the case of the US extended discretionary fiscal stimulus packages were Australia, Britain, China, France, India, Japan and New Zealand. The way was led by the IMF, which called for countries to take measures that are equivalent to 2 per cent of GDP. The European Commission, the guardian of the EU's Monetary and Stability Pact, called on member states to announce fiscal packages of 1.5 percent of GDP. The OECD has also endorsed fiscal stimulus measures. The one country that was initially egregious in its opposition to fiscal measures was Germany, whose then SPD finance minister, Peer Steinbrück, dismissed such packages as 'crass Keynesianism'.

Given the revival of interest in the use of fiscal policy, economists will certainly have plenty of opportunity to study its effects and to identify what works and what does not. The first evidence of that work is beginning to become available. The Congressional Budget Office has looked at the effects on output of the 2008 tax rebates and the effect of President Obama's American Recovery and Reinvestment Act. The CBO had expected 40 per cent of President

How effective is fiscal policy in demand management terms?

Bush's tax cut to be spent within six months, cumulatively raising consumption by 2.5 per cent. Some household surveys of direct consumer behaviour such as use of credit cards suggest that about a third of the tax rebate was spent. However, other surveys of households, where people answer questions, suggest that only 20 per cent of the tax rebate was spent. The CBO estimates that the 2009 fiscal stimulus raised the level of GDP by between 1.7 and 4.2 per cent and lowered unemployment by between 0.7 and 1.5 percentage points. The CBO research note estimates that in 2009 increased Federal government expenditure increased GDP cumulatively by 2.5 per cent.

It is probably too early to come to any definite conclusions about the effectiveness of the fiscal measures taken during the credit crunch and what some economists are now calling the Second Great Contraction. The different research methodologies mentioned above are yielding different results, and while some approaches such as looking at what consumers did with their credit cards suggest they spent tax rebates, the method based on answers to survey questions suggesting that the bulk the stimulus was saved can be matched to data recording an aggregate rise in the level of the US savings ratio that took place at the same time. What is significant about this literature and debate in the US is that it illustrates the vigour, range and rigour of the public policy debate compared to that in the UK.

What is clear is that active fiscal policies that go above and beyond accommodating the operation of the normal so-called automatic stabilisers should neither result in a permanent increase in public expenditure nor a permanent increase in the budget deficit. In political and practical policy terms, that is a genuine challenge. Even the operation of automatic stabilisers and 'recession'-related spending has a habit of permanently entrenching itself and raising expenditure over the cycle. The criteria for judging a well-constructed fiscal stimulus package are: targeted, timely and temporary. Policy makers find it difficult to meet the 'temporary' criterion.

Sorry, We Have No Money

Chapter 4: Can sovereign states go bust?

THE CRISIS IN THE BANKING SYSTEM between 2007 and 2009 was stabilised by governments socialising the banks' losses and ensuring that the principal risks of the banking system were transferred to the collective responsibility of taxpayers. This had the effect of stabilising the banking system but raising testing and potentially awkward questions about the stability of governments as sovereign creditors. When governments borrow they are in a different position from other debtors. It is often said that sovereign borrowers cannot go bankrupt. Governments that control the central bank of the currency that they have borrowed in, can finance their debts by monetising them, which implies their real value will be liquidated by inflation. Where a government actually defaults, creditors' rights are less well protected. Their legal rights are limited because many assets are immune from legal action and a court judgment is more difficult to enforce against a recalcitrant sovereign entity. In that sense sovereign borrowers are not subject to conventional bankruptcy and insolvency procedures. Historically there have, however, been many examples of sovereign borrowers defaulting on their debts. Carmen M Reinhart and Kenneth Rogoff explore these episodes of financial crisis and default in 'This Time is Different: Eight Centuries of Financial Folly', the book they published in 2010 just after the recent credit crisis. They catalogue the many examples of governments defaulting on their obligations. They also explore how periods of rapid growth in bank lending, rising house and other asset prices generate quasi, or temporary and unsustainable tax revenues and spending. When the bubbles burst there is a protracted adjustment and a cluster of financial crises and they show how problems in banking systems can spill over and undermine the fiscal position of governments. The book was published at roughly the time the financial markets were starting to look at the solvency of government borrowing, which led to a full-blown sovereign debt crisis inside the euro-zone.

The bond markets that lend money to governments are normally concerned about three risks: inflation, repayment, and the market

Can sovereign states go bust?

risk that interest rates may go up, thereby reducing the value of bonds on the secondary market. The market risk that interest rates may change and devalue investors' bond portfolios is really a function the fixed income markets' assessment of inflation risks, the demand for government bonds within investors' portfolios and assessments about the capacity of governments to service their debts in the long term out of taxation.

Normally the least pressing risk in relation to government borrowing is credit risk. Or to be more precise, when governments borrow in their own currency, credit risk is much reduced, because of their power to extract resources from taxation or if that fails to monetise government debt through inflation. Given the perception that sovereign borrowers cannot go bankrupt, economists sometimes refer to US Treasury bonds and UK gilts in a shorthand way as 'risk free' assets. Although government bond holders learnt to their cost in the 20th century that while governments may not go bust they can preside over inflation that liquidates the real value of the debt they owe. Much of the so-called equity investment culture that has dominated professional fund management since the late 1950s can be attributed to the effects of protracted 'creeping' peacetime inflation on the real value of government debt both in the UK and in the US which caused the classic 'trustee' type of investor such as a pension fund or a university to turn from principally investing in government bonds to investing in equities. In the late 1950s when the Church of England Commissioners announced that they would no longer invest principally in gilt edged securities, the position was pithily expressed by the Cambridge monetary economist Sir Dennis Robertson that 'when you cannot fool the Church of England any more, you cannot fool anyone'. Bond markets showed that they would not necessarily absorb increasing supplies of government bonds at what before had been the normal long-term rate of interest on government debt. In the last forty years of the 20th century 'fixed' income markets became volatile as investors responded to progressively higher and unstable rates of inflation in the 1970s and the periods of disinflation that followed in the 1980s and 1990s.

In the 1970s the British gilt market showed that even for sovereign creditors borrowing in their own currencies, with the added assistance of foreign exchange controls, governments faced genuine constraints on the amount that they could borrow at an acceptable price. And that government borrowing in a domestic capital market could crowd out private sector borrowing. Indeed there was a brief incident when the British government could not sell the gilts that it wanted to, which at the time was described as the 'Gilt Strike'. Although in truth the main lesson from the 1970s, despite the dire condition of the UK's public finances and all its other economic problems such as very high inflation, was the UK's capacity to borrow, albeit at an increasing cost.

While sovereign borrowers in their own currency may not go bankrupt in the conventional way, governments borrowing in currencies other than their own paper or fiat currency can go bankrupt and have done so. Canadian provinces are sovereign borrowers, but they have no control over the currencies they choose to borrow in. They have little choice other than to extract the necessary taxes to service the debt, although there are circumstances where this may be beyond their capacity. In 1936 the Province of Alberta was forced to default on its debt. Four years previously an independent country had found itself in the same position. The Dominion of Newfoundland, then an independent country, could not service its debts, defaulted and suspended its democratic constitution and handed its government over to a special Royal Commission sent from London.

The UK itself, while proudly boasting of having never missed an interest or principal payment on its gilts, is less comfortable exploring how it defaulted in December 1932 on the US dollar debts it incurred to the US government during the First World War. I once had the unfortunate experience of meeting a US Treasury official who had the responsibility of calculating the outstanding

Can sovereign states go bust?

interest owed on the debt for the US General Accounting Office. He wasted no time in asking when me we were going to pay back the money we owed the US.

A European Central Bank (ECB) research paper by Ludger Schunecht, Jurgen von Hagen and Guido Wolswijk, 'Government Risk Premiums in the Bond Market: EMU and Canada' (2008) explored the analogous position of the Canadian provinces and the member states in the euro-zone. Looking at risk premiums and the effects of fiscal equalisation, the lesson that the paper drew was that in Canada provinces that receive money under the federal government's fiscal equalisation arrangements appeared to be able to borrow at slightly reduced risk premiums and do not pay a penalty in higher borrowing costs for the fact that they receive transfers when they run budget deficits. The larger provinces that pay into the federal equalisation scheme are penalised by bond markets when they run large deficits. Drawing on their results for borrowing costs by regional borrowers in Canada and Germany, their conclusion was that fiscal support allows sub-national governments to borrow at more favourable terms, with the implication that the markets believe that such governments will obtain assistance if they need it. This means that governments can accumulate debts that they may not be able to service or manage.

Sovereign borrowers that are members of the euro-zone do not have control over their domestic currency. The governments of Greece, Portugal and Spain are in a position similar to that of the Canadian Province of Alberta. The crisis in the euro-zone prompted by Greece in May 2010 arose because the bond markets woke up to this obvious fact which they had ignored during the first eleven years of the euro-zone created in 1999. The May 2010 crisis was a full-blown financial crisis. The European interbank market seized up and Greece could not borrow to roll over its debt. The crisis was aggravated because the Maastricht Treaty expressly prohibited member states being bailed out by the European Central Bank, while at the same time the political leaders of the countries

Sorry, We Have No Money

involved maintained the nonsense conceit that the euro-zone was some kind of no default zone as well as a single currency zone with a prohibition on bailouts. The fundamental principles of the euro-zone were then breached when the Council of Ministers announced the creation of a €750 billion fund to assist countries such as Greece. €500 billion was from the members of the euro-zone and €250 billion was from the IMF. It was further and significantly more undermined when the ECB announced that it would purchase Greek government bonds to stabilise their value. This decision was motivated by a desire to avoid falls in the value of Greek bonds, undermining the capital base of European banks that was already weak. European banks were estimated to hold €68 billion of Greek debt. A central bank purchasing government bonds to stabilise their nominal market value is the classic case of a central bank monetising government debt. It is what the Reichsbank started to do in Germany in 1917, which eventually led to the Weimar Republic's hyperinflation. The ECB, however, was careful to announce that it would 'sterilise' the impact of these bond purchases by withdrawing other liquidity from the euro-zone to prevent a loosening of monetary conditions. How effective such sterilisation could be over a protracted period is a difficult question to answer.

The Greek crisis and the broader crisis in the euro-zone illustrates how even sovereign borrowers encounter practical constraints. And how even when a sovereign borrower such as the UK has control over its own currency, monetising its debt creates immense problems and carries with it real risks. The larger the stock of debt and the more of it that has to be regularly refinanced the more vulnerable a sovereign borrower is. The lesson for Britain is that a sensible country does not want to go there. Running deficits in excess of the trend rate of growth at the peak of the economic cycle as the Labour Chancellor of the Exchequer Gordon Brown did between 2004 and 2006, with the budget deficit averaging each year over 3 per cent of GDP, means that debt is accumulated in relation to national income when it should be reduced. Maintaining high deficits

Can sovereign states go bust?

for years as a semi-permanent feature of fiscal policy rather than for just a few years during an intense adverse economic shock creates a level of debt that is progressively more difficult to manage and limits the capacity of the state to respond to other future economic, environmental and political risks.

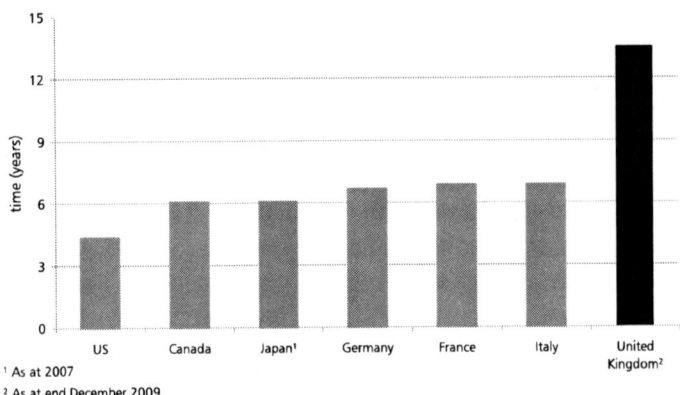

¹ As at 2007
² As at end December 2009

FIGURE 4.1: *G7 debt maturity in 2008 (Source: OECD, HM Treasury Debt Management Office)*

In some respects the UK is better placed to manage these risks than other advanced OECD economies. There is a large domestic capital market and a strong demand for long dated gilts from insurance companies and pensions funds. The average maturity of UK government debt is about thirteen and a half years. That is twice as long as the average maturity of the debt of G7 countries (see Figure 4.1). And historically investors have shown themselves willing to lend to Britain in even the direst circumstances of war and inflation (despite the awkward incident of the 'Gilt Strike'). Yet the UK should not be complacent. Modern financial markets are both myopic and unpredictable. They ignore the obvious and then concentrate on it with an almost bipolar neurosis that cannot be assuaged or easily tempered. The UK is one of several mature economies that

Sorry, We Have No Money

bond market investors potentially have in their sights. The risk that the UK runs, now that its stock of public debt is set to peak at over 70 per cent of GDP and it has a structural budget deficit of around 6 or 7 per cent of GDP, if the Coalition had not taken radical action in the Emergency Budget, is that the financial markets could apply their attention to it and drive long-term interest rates much higher to reflect an appropriate risk premium. That would make the cost of private sector capital in the UK much more expensive and would lead to a slower rate of capital accumulation and a reduced growth rate in the medium term. In order to avoid that sort of unwelcome attention the Coalition government was right to take action. The US has a highly unstable medium-term fiscal position. There is a danger that, in order to explore the US position, the bond markets may have chosen to 'practice' on the UK. The credit rating agencies would consider downgrading the UK, as a practice run before turning their attention properly to the US. The Emergency Budget in 2010 should ensure that will not now happen.

Historically during war Britain has borrowed heavily. In the 1950s after the impact of two world wars the stock of public debt in relation to GDP was 275 per cent. This imposed a huge burden on the British economy. It was managed by constraining the private domestic consumption of households in the manner that Keynes set out in his 1939 pamphlet 'How to Pay for the War' and through an extended peacetime inflation that turned into rapidly accelerating, high and unstable levels of inflation in the 1970s. In the 1940s and 1950s British people paid for the debt with direct controls on their living standards. Petrol, car purchase and sweets were all rationed for an extended period in peacetime. The tax burden was heavy. In the 1960s and 1970s inflation brought different problems. The fundamental working of the price mechanism was undermined and the administrative controls on wages and prices introduced to ameliorate the symptoms of price inflation did huge damage to company balance sheets and the proper functioning of the labour market. In the 1970s profits collapsed and a genuine Marxian crisis of capitalism was created. This crisis was acknowledged for what it was by Marxist economists such as the late Andrew Glyn and Bob Sutcliffe in their provocative book 'British Capitalism, Workers and the Profits Squeeze' (1972). The lesson of the post-war episode is not that high debts are fundable, but that they impose huge costs on an economy and make the conduct of monetary policy much more difficult. Going through all those things was certainly worthwhile to finance the destruction of the Nazi regime in Germany; whether such burdens would secure similar levels of political support to maintain current levels of public sector pay, pension rights and other transfer payments such as the structure of tax credits introduced in 1998 is another question. Governments can borrow, but debt is not burdenless. Britain does not face bankruptcy, but does have to recognise that it will encounter constraints on its future consumption if it does not reduce its level of government borrowing in relation to GDP.

Chapter 5: Public sector efficiency in the UK

THERE ARE CLEAR BENEFITS FROM A PUBLIC SECTOR that is much larger than the one that existed at the start of the 20th century. Collectively provided and financed goods and services makes sense. In many respects a developed and properly functioning welfare state is a powerful adjunct to a dynamic market economy. It corrects not just market failures in specific markets such as asymmetries of information and adverse selection that make it difficult to have properly functioning markets in things such as health care, but it helps to modify an uneven dispersion of income that is inherent in a market economy. By remedying the defects of the price system and the uneven distribution of incomes that results, the public sector and the welfare state support the successful operation of the market economy.

While the public sector is there to remedy the failures of the market, there is also plenty of scope for public sector failure. Allocating resources outside the framework of the price mechanism presents an immediate problem of how to maintain economic efficiency. This problem was recognised by socialist economists from the start of the growth of the welfare state in the first part of the 20th century. Economists such as Abba Lerner devoted a lot of time to thinking about ways of replicating the disciplines and efficiency of the market within a socialist framework of planning and resources allocation.

Fundamental efficiency challenge in public services

THE PUBLIC SECTOR, because it does not face a hard budget constraint when using resources, is exposed to agency problems and rent seeking from both political interest groups and from producer groups that are employed by it. As public sectors expanded in the 20th century there was increasing evidence of public sector failure as well as market failure. Public sector bodies often used resources inefficiently and were distinguished by large losses of what the Harvard economist Harvey Leibenstein called X-efficiency (see

Chapter 11, 'The neo-classical analytical paradigm') as well as egregious examples of producer interests taking precedence over other concerns.

Value for money and public sector reform

IN THE 1970S AND 1980S genuine concern about the efficiency of the public sector combined with the need to reduce public expenditure as a share of national income, both to reduce public borrowing and to ensure that the public sector did not crowd out the private sector, resulted in squeezes in public sector pay, capital investment and the overall share of national income taken by public spending. Public expenditure in the UK was subjected to a succession of financial control and efficiency initiatives in order to increase its productivity and control its costs. These ranged from cash limits and the Prime Minister's 'Value for Money' initiatives, the review of public expenditure carried out by the former managing director of Marks & Spencer Lord Rayner, to the development of the internal market in NHS health spending and the citizen's charter launched by John Major. By the early 1990s the UK public sector had been subjected to every conceivable efficiency and reinvention of government reform conceivable. Yet there remained obvious concerns about the quality and efficiency of the principal public services.

New Labour: spend, spend, spend

IN 1997 THE NEW LABOUR PROJECT, while employing the rhetoric of prudence to great effect, decisively broke with the previous twenty years of public expenditure control. Public expenditure was seen as investment and starting in 1998 there were discretionary increases in almost all areas of public expenditure, with the obvious exception of defence spending. The fundamental judgment that this was based on was that Britain's public services would significantly improve if the amount of resources deployed in them was increased. This judgment was not only shared by Labour ministers and their Whitehall officials, but was, to paraphrase Jane Austen, a truth almost universally held throughout the public services from the trade unions to the most senior local authority managers and indeed most Treasury officials themselves. The mood was pithily summarised by one former Treasury Permanent Secretary: 'As long as certain services such as health and education were principally provided and funded by the state, these programmes had to be properly funded and if that meant a larger ratio of public expenditure within national income, so be it'.

The Treasury also presented this judgment to the international bodies that take a serious interest in the UK economy and its public finances. These are the EU Commission, which has responsibility for monitoring member states' borrowing and fiscal policies under the Maastricht Treaty, the OECD and the IMF, which produces annual assessments of member states' economies. They were persuaded that increased public expenditure in the UK was justified, and the accompanying borrowing was justified because of a long period when public services had been under-resourced. These bodies normally respond to pressures from important member state governments and are reluctant to publish reports that touch sensitive spots. The OECD and IMF produced happy glosses on the UK fiscal policy that largely went against the advice normally offered to other governments. As the consequences of the huge increases in spending became apparent, these organisations increasingly expressed reservations about the rate of the increase in spending. Two principal matters were raised: the IMF expressed concern that the UK's fiscal rules provided no effective constraint on public expenditure growth; and the OECD worried about the capacity of the public sector to make efficient use of such rapid increases in resources without an increase in the public sector cost base.

Public sector efficiency in the UK

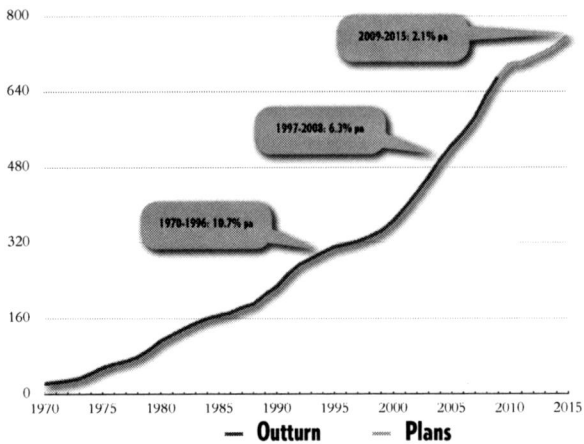

FIGURE 5.1: *Total managed expenditure, 1970–2015, cash (£ billion) (Source: HM Treasury)*

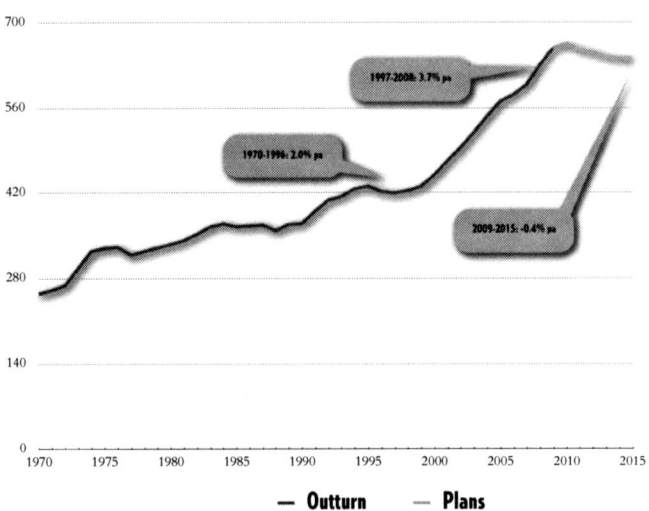

FIGURE 5.2: *Total managed expenditure, 1970–2015, real (£ billion, 2008-09 prices) (Source: HM Treasury)*

Sorry, We Have No Money

Measuring public sector output in the national accounts

IN MANY RESPECTS the UK has offered the international community an almost laboratory experiment in exploring the cost, consequences and benefits of large and rapid increases in public spending. In the past there would have been little serious or rigorous attempt to measure the outcomes and productivity of the additional spending on public services. As it happens, as a result of a revolution in national accounting conventions that the EU obliged the UK government to make, that took effect in 1998, the way statisticians approach measuring public sector output within GDP changed. These changes were highly technical and of little interest even to economists unless they took a specialist interest in national accounting. They represented a huge upheaval in the system of national accounts, first developed by the Cambridge economist Sir Richard Stone in the 1940s to provide the British government and Lord Keynes, in particular, with the necessary information to enable the economy to be fully mobilised for war.

The changes obliged statisticians to measure often difficult things that in the past they had not taken account of, such as crime, largely because it is difficult to obtain reliable information on it, in addition to conceptual issues such as whether illegal activity could increase output and economic welfare. Big changes were also made to the treatment of capital goods, from computers to farmyard animals. Until the new system was introduced in 1998 public sector output was assumed to be equal to its input. So an increase in public expenditure was automatically recorded as an increase in GDP output. This new system of European System of Accounts required that public output should instead be measured directly. This later evolved into a binding condition for all EU member states to implement direct volume measures into their national accounts.

The argument for making this change was that by valuing output as equal to input, measured output from the public sector could only ever grow at the same rate as its input. This had three un-wanted implications: measured productivity growth is always zero because productivity is calculated as the ratio of outputs to in-puts; increases in real expenditure are self justifying as they always produce equal increases in outputs; and technology improvements that reduce production costs cause both input and output to fall when output may be unaffected. There were reasons why some economists interested in national accounting were suspicious of this change. Measuring the output of the public services is difficult and there was a real danger that the level of GDP being produced by the public sector could be in effect massaged up.

	Average annual rate of growth (%)	Share of growth in TME (%)
Health	6.0	24.7
Education	4.6	15.4
Social protection	2.9	26.0
Local government	2.1	9.6
Average	3.7	

TABLE 5.1: *Total managed expenditure by function 1997–2009 (Source: HM Treasury)*

The row: public sector productivity falls

WHEN, HOWEVER, THE ONS PRODUCED its first substantial piece of work that directly measured the outcomes and productivity of UK public services in 2003 ('Understanding Government Out-put and Productivity') it provoked a serious political row, because it enabled the Shadow Chancellor Michael Howard to assert in a forensic manner that public sector productivity had collapsed. The publication immediately exposed a serious issue of public sec-tor inefficiency. This was followed by a slow-burning argument, if not row, over the next two years where Labour ministers were inconvenienced by having to explain why the ONS showed that huge increases in spending had not been matched by comparable increases in service. The statisticians had entered a political mine-field, albeit a highly technical one. This work turned out to be so contentious that the Warden of Nuffield College Oxford, Sir Tony Atkinson, an economist, whose principal area of interest is in the distribution of income and wealth, was asked to conduct an inquiry into these difficult issues. The Atkinson Review resulted in the UK Centre for the Management of Government Activity being set up within the ONS in July 2005. An additional and advisory board was set up to offer advice and monitor progress and a number of advisory panels were set up. These include health, education and children and defence.

Atkinson Review

THE ATKINSON REVIEW set out two broad principles for this work and made nine specific technical recommendations about how the measurement of public sector output could be improved. Measurement of the public sector should as far as possible follow the parallel procedures used for measuring market output; and the output of the government sector should be measured taking account of an adjustment for equability. The technical recommendations covered areas such as widening the coverage of output volume indicators, and improvements to the deflators used in the measurement of the volume of public spending and productivity.

As a result of this work and political pressure the ONS has changed its estimate of UK GDP and raised it by 5 per cent between 1995 and 2005. Despite these revisions to the methodology and the consequent upward revision of the identified output, this work on public sector output and productivity provides a serious indictment of the efficiency of UK public expenditure. What the work shows is that between 1997 and 2007 there has been an increase in public sector inputs. Output increased, but the rate of increase in output was at a slower rate than the inputs and productivity has roughly halved.

Public expenditure in 2007 accounted for over 40 per cent of GDP and about half that spending goes directly on public services such as health and education as opposed to transfer payments on items such as social security benefits and debt interest payments. Spending on public services accounts for over 20 per cent of GDP. In the period between 1997 and 2007 the output of total public services rose by 33.6 per cent. This equates to an annual average growth in output of 2.9 per cent. Over the same period GDP rose by an annual average of 2.9 per cent, while volumes of inputs used to provide these services grew by 38 per cent, or an annual average increase of 3.3 per cent. As a result, total public service productivity fell over the period by 3.2 per cent, an annual average fall in productivity of 0.3 per cent (see Figure 5.3).

United Kingdom
Percentage change from 1997

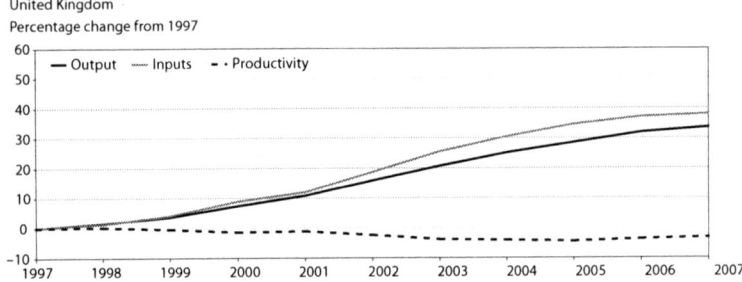

FIGURE 5.3: *Total public service output, inputs and productivity estimates, 1997-2007 (Source: Office for National Statistics, UKCeMGA)*

There have been some significant changes in the composition of public spending on services since 1997. This is reflected in the weight given to different services within the General Government Final Consumption Expenditure Index. Between 1997 and 2007 spending on health rose from 27.6 to 31.5 per cent, education from 18.8 to 19.3 per cent, adult social care from 5.8 to 6.4 per cent and children in care from 1.9 to 2.4 per cent. However, spending on public order and safety and the police barely changed and defence fell from 15.1 to 11 per cent (see Table 5.2).

	Health care	Education	Adult Social Care	Social Security Admin	Children Social Care	Public Order & Safety	Police	Defence	Other	Total
1997	27.6	18.8	5.8	2.2	1.9	4.3	5.5	15.1	18.8	100.0
1998	28.4	18.8	5.9	2.1	2.0	4.2	5.5	14.3	18.8	100.0
1999	28.8	18.7	5.9	2.2	2.1	4.5	5.4	13.2	19.2	100.0
2000	28.5	18.8	6.0	2.3	2.0	4.7	5.2	13.6	18.9	100.0
2001	29.0	19.2	5.9	2.0	2.1	4.5	5.6	12.4	19.3	100.0
2002	29.1	19.5	6.1	1.9	2.1	4.4	5.6	12.3	19.0	100.0
2003	29.3	19.1	6.3	2.2	2.2	4.5	5.5	12.4	18.4	100.0
2004	30.0	19.0	6.4	2.1	2.3	4.5	5.5	11.6	18.7	100.0
2005	30.1	18.9	6.5	2.2	2.3	4.5	5.5	11.1	18.9	100.0
2006	31.0	18.9	6.4	1.6	2.4	4.3	5.4	11.8	18.2	100.0
2007	31.5	19.3	6.4	1.5	2.4	4.2	5.5	11.0	18.1	100.0

TABLE 5.2: *General government final consumption expenditure weights by service[1], 1997–2007 (Source: Office for National Statistics, UKCeMGA)*

The striking feature of the ONS study of public sector output and productivity is that the services most favoured have performed least well. Spending on health care rose by 59.3 per cent, children's social care by 74.3 per cent and education by 29.6 per cent. Health-care productivity fell by 4.3 per cent between 1997 and 2007, at an annual average compound rate of 0.4 per cent. Adult social care productivity fell by 4.3 per cent, an annual average fall of 0.4 per

---

1 Includes that part of further education dealing with under-19s.

Public sector efficiency in the UK

cent. Productivity in education fell by 3.2 per cent at an annual average rate of 0.3 per cent. The largest fall in productivity was in children's social care, which fell by 20.9 per cent, an annual average fall of 2.4 per cent.

The headline fall in productivity in children's services may need to be treated with caution. Half of this spending is measured directly. It includes the cost of looked-after children. Spending on this has fallen as local authorities have made increasing use of family settings rather than expensive children's homes. As a result, more looked-after children are being placed in foster and adoption family settings and an increase in quality may have taken place that may not have been fully recognised in the adjusted output measure. While the child protection services portion of that area of spending is still measured in the input-output way, so that a large increase in spending definition implies no increase in productivity. In addition, there may have been some improvement in the quality of care of children being fostered that was not picked up, it is not at all clear that the increase in children's spending that was not directly measured merely clothed a further fall in productivity.

Comparative health spending and efficiency within the UK

THE IMPLICATION THAT THERE IS NOT a straightforward connection between the level of public spending on a service and the level or quality of that service is clear. Moreover, the broad thrust of the implications of the ONS work on public sector output tallies with other studies and other less systematic information that we have about the UK public sector. The Nuffield Trust study of health care spending that looks at the performance of England and the devolved territories within the UK tells a striking story. The devolved administrations in Scotland, Wales and Northern Ireland all spend more on health than England, have more doctors, nurses and managers per head than England, yet it is England that delivers more patient treatment, appears to have higher productivity and lower waiting lists.

When comparisons are made between Scotland and North East England which have similar populations, income, deprivation and health status the contrast is stark. In 2006 Scotland spent 6 per cent per head more than the North East of England on health care, but the North East recorded 18 per cent more outpatient attendances, almost 40 per cent more day cases and 50 per cent more inpatient admissions, with lower ratios of staff per patient. The report suggests that Scotland appeared to exhibit producer capture,[2] with doctors and nurses being sheltered from challenge about what they did. One of its authors, Professor Gwyn Bevan, concluded that extra money given to Scotland 'appears to have allowed staff to have an easier life'. The Nuffield Trust study only looked at measurable outcomes from identifiable hospital activity such as operations and outpatients visits, rather than family doctor performance. Hospital activity may not be a perfect measure of health care; Scottish Executive ministers argued that their primary care is so good it keeps patients out of hospital, explaining the low activity rates. Yet if Scottish primary care is so good at keeping people out of hospital, why does Scotland have such a large and expensive hospital workforce, with more beds per head, more hospital doctors and more nurses than England, but still lower rates of activity?

NHS consultants' pay and GP contracts

THE DEPARTMENT OF 'HEALTH agreed that a new national pay contract would be negotiated for NHS medical consultants in

---

2   Producer group capture takes place where the producers of a good or service have a high stake in the rewards paid for producing it and distort the production cost in the interest of the people being paid to provide it, rather than for the benefit of the people who are paying either directly or as taxpayers to receive it.

England, which took effect in 2003. Consultants are the grade of senior specialist doctors that work in hospitals. Their pay was based on the arrangements originally agreed between the BMA and Aneurin Bevan in 1948. The need for a new contract was set out in the NHS Plan 2000 as part of a wider pay modernisation agenda intended to recruit more and better paid staff working differently and presumably more productively. The Department of Health intended that the new contract should reward consultants through better pay and increased recognition for their NHS work. Employing hospitals in return would get greater control and management of their consultants' workload. Patients would benefit from a more flexible and responsive service. The Department hoped to reward those consultants who made the greatest contribution to NHS work by increasing their pay and reducing the average number of hours worked per consultant, and in return consultants would increase their productivity. These benefits would only come about after the introduction of compulsory and rigorous process of workload planning for each individual hospital consultant.

The House of Commons Public Accounts Committee reported on the implementation of the new contract in 'Pay Modernisation: A new contract for NHS consultants in England' (2007). It concluded that the implementation of the contract was rushed and the NHS had yet to see many of the mooted benefits. Over the first three years the Department of Health allocated an additional £715 billion so that NHS trusts could fund it. That is £150 million more than was originally estimated as necessary to fund it. The employing hospitals still believed that the contract had been underfunded by the Department of Health. Consultants' pay increased on average by 27 per cent from £86,746 to £109,974. Their working hours decreased and there was no measurable improvement in productivity. There was an increase in the number of consultants working in the NHS, although that was already a rising trend before the introduction of the new contract. The number of hours consultants worked in private practice neither increased nor fell significantly.

Sorry, We Have No Money

The other intended benefits failed to materialise. The proportion of time spent by consultants on direct clinical care is less than intended and the contract has not been used to extend and develop new services for patients. It is hard to avoid the conclusion that the new consultant contract represents a practical example of the implied warning given by the OECD to the British government that rapid increases in public spending may not result in higher output but instead would be absorbed by more rapid inflation.

The Public Accounts Committee has also looked at GP contracts and the provision of out-of-hours care at weekends and in the evenings. Until 2004 GPs the non-specialist family doctors based in the community were responsible for providing this service. They normally did it by either pooling their responsibility through a GP co-operative or delegating it to a commercial deputising service. Responsibility for the service was unpopular among GPs and there were increasing complaints from patients about it. From April 2004 the Department of Health gave GPs the chance to opt out of personal responsibility for the service under a new General Medical Services contract. This enabled the GP to give up an average of £6,000 a year and the local Primary Care Trust took over responsibility for out-of-hours care. The Public Accounts Committee in 'The Provision of Out-of-Hours Care in England' (2007) found that preparations for the new service were 'shambolic both at the national and the local level'. The Department of Health took part in the negotiation of the new General Medical Services contract only as an observer and 'only the doctors did well out of the deal on out-of-hours costs'. The service had started to improve but 'the actual performance against key access targets is still not good enough'. The percentage of providers meeting targets for 'call answering, definitive clinical assessment and consultation times is extremely low.' And the new service was £70 million more expensive than foreseen.

Children's care services

LARGE AMOUNTS OF money have been spent on improving children's services through initiatives such as Quality Protects, Sure Start and the Every Child Matters programmes. It is not clear how well focused and successful these policies have been. They duplicated work already being done by local authority children's social services and organisations such as the health visitor service. The Public Accounts Committee's report 'Sure Start Children's Centres' (2007) showed the scale and ambition of the Sure Start programme. Until 2006 the Department for Education and Skills spent £2.1 billion on Sure Start local programmes, and then transferred responsibility for them to local authorities and allocated a budget of £1.8 billion to help. In September 2006 there were around 1,000 Sure Start centres and local authorities were given responsibility for more than trebling that number to 3,500 by 2010. The Public Accounts Committee drew attention to the need to improve financial management, the lack of understanding of what their unit costs are and that there was limited evidence that spending was applied where it was most needed. The Department for Education was slow to produce guidance on performance measurement and monitoring. The report also made a wider point that under Local Area Agreements that gave more local freedom to move resources between services, it was also important to have 'robust local systems to measure performance that should undederpin assessments of cost effectiveness'. Most of the research on Sure Start has been soft focus research and has not addressed the concerns that the Public Accounts Committee has about unit costs and financial management.

Education standards and quality

EDUCATION SPENDING HAS INCREASED hugely. Overall education and training spending has risen by over £50 billion from £38.6 billion in 1997-98 to £89.2 billion in 2010-11, which represents a real terms increase of 70 per cent. Yet it is not at all clear that this spending has been matched by a comparable improvement in educational standards. I do not have strong views on the issues of educational standards, but I have attempted to summarise some of the issues in the present debate to illustrate the fact it would be naive to assert that there has been a straightforward connection between higher public spending on educational standards and improvements in education.

The debate about education spending turns on the quality of the results. This debate was well summarised by Jack Grimston, the education correspondent of the *Sunday Times* in 'The £100 billion schools scandal' (24 January 2010). There is an extensive debate about the value of the qualifications that students have been gaining at 16 and 18. The Head Master of Harrow, Barnaby Lenon, has warned that these qualifications should not allow us to be deceived into thinking that children 'especially children from poorer homes', may be getting 'worthless qualifications.' There appears to have been an inflation of grades. In 2009 26.7 per cent of A levels were awarded as A grades. Robert Coe, Reader in Education at Durham University, tracks the value of grades by comparing pupils' results with their performance in a series of tests that are kept constant in their difficulty from year to another. Coe's conclusion is that 'the grades have gone up but the amount you have to do to get each grade has clearly gone down'. Coe estimates that at A level there has been 'a steady slide of a grade a year over the past twenty years in terms of what you get for what you do'. His conclusion is that a student who would have received a B grade in 1997 would now receive an A.

Coe's judgment about grade inflation is challenged by parts of the education producer establishment. John Dunford, the general secretary of the association of school teachers and college lecturers, told the *Sunday Times* when it reported Coe's research that the 'debate around exam results is false' and there is 'no evidence of a decline in standards' in the exam system. Dunford argues that what has happened is that the education and exam system has moved from preparing an elite to run a society to the public expectation that a very large number of people will gain good qualifications. Yet employers and college and university teachers who have to use or teach people with qualifications express concern about their reliability and quality. One employer, Calumet Photographic of Milton Keynes that employs 150 people to sell photographic equipment to professional photographers, is sufficiently unhappy with the basic spelling and arithmetic of job applicants that it has introduced a special test for them. Managing director Michele Channer explained to the *Sunday Times* that 'the standards of education we see are often unfortunately below those suggested by the exams on the CVs'. In the past it would have been relatively easy to dismiss such employer complaints and anecdotal. Yet Sir Mike Tomlinson the former chief schools' inspector told the *Sunday Times* that such concerns were justified, saying that 'it is reasonable for employers to assume that if you get a grade A to C in GCSE maths you have a grasp of basic functional skills. The fact is, that is not an assurance I can give. We have found students at grades A to C who failed basic numeracy tests. When employers complain, they have a legitimate basis for complaint.'

University teachers have complained for many years that students have less knowledge of core subjects such as maths, natural sciences and languages than they did thirty years before. The *Sunday Times* was told by Phil Langdon, a lecturer in physiology at Bristol University, that he was repeatedly having trouble getting concepts across when discussing simple numerical problems with students. One example that Langdon told the *Sunday Times* about regarded basic numeracy: 'I had four first year medical students who between them could not decide how many centimetres could be in a metre. They suggested it might be 1,000'.

This summary of concerns put together by the *Sunday Times* about educational standards is consistent with the ONS data raising issues about productivity within education and suggests that to

Sorry, We Have No Money

dismiss the ONS findings, because the statisticians cannot measure improved quality, is misleading. Moreover, the ONS work is also consistent with work done by the National Audit Office and the House of Commons Public Accounts Committee.

The Public Accounts Committee investigated maths teaching in primary schools in 'Mathematics Performance in primary schools: getting the best results' (2009). The report shows that there has been a National Strategy to improve mathematics in primary schools since the late 1990s. By 2007-08 the strategy had cost £104 million. Its objective was to raise performance through extensive teacher and learning resources, supported by professional development programmes for teachers. In 2006-07 £2.3 billion was spent on maths teaching out of total expenditure of £10 billion on primary school teaching and teaching support staff. Despite this expenditure, improvements in mathematics results in primary schools levelled off from 2000. In 2008 79 per cent of Key Stage 2 11-year-old pupils achieved the government's expected standard. These were the highest recorded results but failed to meet the Department for Education's ambitions of 85 per cent meeting the test standard by 2006. It meant that over a fifth of secondary school students began their secondary education without a secure foundation in mathematics. A central problem is the 'lack of depth in subject knowledge of many primary school teachers and the lack of take up of continuing professional development in mathematics' which are concerns that the Department for Education had only recently begun to address well into a ten-year programme.

'Skills for Life: Progress in Improving Adult Literacy and Numeracy' (2009) is a Public Accounts Committee report that deals with the £5 billion spent between 2001 and 2007 on basic skills. In 2003 75 per cent of the adult population of working age had numeracy skills below a good GCSE pass and 56 per cent had literacy skills below that level. In 2007 the government announced a new objective to help 95 per cent of the adult population of working age to achieve functional literacy and numeracy by 2020. If that objective were to be achieved, however, that would only place the UK in the top 25 per cent of the OECD member countries. The targets for literacy and numeracy will be difficult to achieve. There are particular problems with the numeracy targets because of the lack of numeracy teachers. Moreover, while many people with poor literacy and numeracy skills come into contact with a range of government services, such as Jobcentre Plus, the Prison and Probation services, the take-up of courses is relatively small in percentage terms. Only one in five offenders with identifiable literacy and numeracy needs were enrolled on courses. The *Sunday Times* article and these Public Accounts Committee reports tell a consistent story that suggests that the large increase in spending on education and training since 1997 has not resulted in a comparable improvement in performance.

UK's ranking falls in OECD study

ONE OF THE PRINCIPAL INTERNATIONAL ATTEMPTS to benchmark educational attainment suggests a patchy record for the UK. The OECD-produced Programme for International Student Assessment (PISA) study shows that far from improving in recent years as a result of higher spending educational attainment have slipped backwards in relative terms. In 2000, UK 15-year-olds were ranked on reading in seventh place, by 2007 it had dropped to seventeenth place. In maths the UK fell from eighth to twenty-fourth and below the international average. In science, secondary school children in the UK dropped from fourth to fourteenth place. Moreover the PISA rankings suggest that there is no obvious connection between a country's ranking in terms of spending on education as a ratio of GDP and measured educational achievements. It is significant that during a period when spending on education significantly increased in the UK, taking it firmly above the OECD average of 5.6 per cent to 5.9 per cent in 2006, the UK's relative performance appeared to fall.

Sorry, We Have No Money

Why did New Labour's spending yield disappointing results?

THE PICTURE THAT EMERGES from the ONS work, the detailed National Audit and Public Account Committee analyses of public spending programmes and the wider public debate is that much of the increased spending from 1997 failed to deliver. Why? Part of the explanation is that the UK already had extensive and expensive public services that had tried to achieve many of the Labour Ministers' ambitions since the 1950s and 1960s. The belief that significant additional resources could somehow transform the performance of these public services was naive. At the margin, the return to using additional resources tends to fall. Diminishing marginal returns is a practical constraint on raising performance simply by adding resources. Some of the new programmes simply duplicated what was already being done.

Sure Start appears to have been inspired by a US Federal government programme called Head Start. This is a programme that funds social services programmes for children in poor local neighbourhoods. It has achieved good results and is much admired. The idea that simply replicating Head Start in the UK would yield similar observable benefits was flawed. In the US there is no comprehensive national welfare state that offers the coherent and systematic provision for children that the UK local authorities, NHS and NHS health visitor service provide. Grafting a version of Head Start onto the existing services already in place in the UK would not deliver comparable benefits at the margin. Sure Start increased pressure on the already over-stretched health visitors and speech therapy services. The Connexions Direct service that replaced the previous careers service and brought together other services was a more expensive way of providing existing services.

Quality Protects was a programme initiated to ensure that local authorities carried out their child protection services properly and improved their focus on preventive work. It provided funding for officers to co-ordinate the Quality Protects agenda across authorities. In practice many local councils that were already doing effective preventive work received additional money for work that was already being done, whereas there were other things that they needed money for. It also resulted in good and effective social work managers being recruited from over-stretched and under-performing departments to become Quality Protects co-ordinators. This took good social services professionals from working directly on services that badly needed their expertise and judgment to better-paid jobs where they were no longer involved in direct case management. A similar dynamic took place with NHS Direct, where many experienced district nurses were recruited to staff its telephone service. Quality Protects illustrated a wider trend where professionals and managers are paid more money and removed from the delivery of front line service. This is similar to the way that inspection services increasingly focus on looking at whole services rather than, for example, concentrating on the regular inspection of services such as residential and nursing care homes where the public are at genuine risk.

It would be very unfair to suggest that all these initiatives were pointless or damaging. The Better Government for Older People programme was an imaginative innovation. NHS Direct was a good idea and should have been developed before, but its implementation resulted in work incentives that made other parts of the health service more difficult. In the judgment of many experienced and realistic public sector managers, more might have been achieved if resources had been channelled through existing services and arrangements for delivering programmes rather than creating new delivery bodies such as Sure Start. Much of the additional money was centrally directed. This means that local authorities and organisations get money for things that are not locally needed yet do not get money for local problems that do not match central spending priorities. The OECD has recognised that a rapid increase in spending may provide the public sector with resources that it cannot easily or swiftly use in a cost-effective manner. The OECD therefore warned that instead of raising public sector output such a rapid increase in spending may instead contribute to an escalation of public sector costs and inflation. This plainly happened and is most evident in increased public sector pay and in the pay of senior public sector managers. A large increase in resources was always likely to result in higher cost inflation and pay, given the continued entrenched professional and producer interest groups in the public sector and the evidently effective influence they continued to wield.

One reason why the increased spending was disappointing in its results was a lack of attention to the need to co-ordinate capital expenditure with current expenditure. More school laboratories in the absence of maths and science teachers will fail to achieve the intended result. Training more doctors, who qualify just at the moment when the Department of Health changes the procedures for employing them, which disrupts previous transitions from study to professional work, and coinciding with a squeeze on hospital trust budgets provoked by deficits in many local hospitals caused by their difficulty in absorbing higher pay costs even within a steeply rising budget, means that less is achieved from the additional spending of medical education than might be expected. This probably reflects the over-centralised character of much of English public expenditure funding and planning, which is particularly pronounced in the NHS.

Public sector trade union power and economic rent seeking

THE PICTURE OF AN EXPENSIVE and relatively inefficient sector that emerges from the ONS and other studies is also confirmed by general evidence on pay, strike action and time lost at work through sickness. These show that average public sector pay is higher than private sector pay. There are more strikes in the public sector than in the private sector and the lion's share of the number of days lost through strike action is in the public sector. The level of strike action reflects much higher levels of trade union membership in the public sector. Employee absence through sickness is around a third higher than in the private sector and an entrenched problem that the government has attempted to reduce with little effect. This combines to form a consistent pattern of producer interests engaging in effective economic rent seeking. At the heart of this is continuing strong trade union power in the public sector. In the 1980s and 1990s effective trade union power diminished significantly in the British private sector; in the public sector it has not. After more than fifteen years this difference in trade union bargaining power is manifested in an identifiable trade union mark-up that is now reflected in public sector pay being higher than in the private sector. This premium in public sector wages over private sector wages remains, even after an adjustment has been made for differences in composition between the private and public sector workforces. Moreover, the pay premium is much magnified when deferred pay in the form of employer-provided pension arrangements are taken into account.

The interesting thing is that the public sector in the UK performs poorly despite having been subjected to a host of different policies by both Conservative and Labour governments over the last thirty years. Increased expenditure has not yielded the benefits that might have been expected and the attempts to measure public sector productivity systematically have generated results that match other less systematic analysis of health spending and educational results. The public sector has not been able to make efficient use of its additional resources.

Sorry, We Have No Money

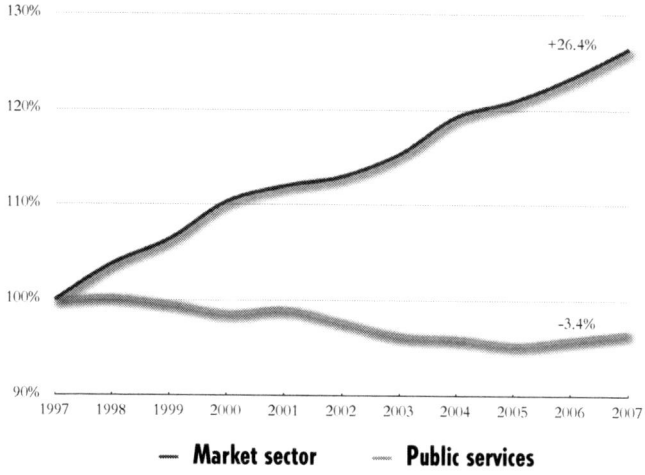

FIGURE 5.4: *Productivity in the market sector and public services, 1997–2007 (Source: HM Treasury)*

Chapter 6: The failure of public sector reform

OVER THE LAST THIRTY YEARS the public sector in the UK has been subject to a range of initiatives to improve its efficiency and value for money. These have ranged from cash limits to the creation of quasi markets with shadow prices. While many of these were worthwhile in themselves, this process of continuous reform has not been able to overcome the fundamental impediments that hinder efficiency in collectively provided goods and services. Some of the reforms themselves, such as contracting out, simply changed the framework in which losses of X-efficiency and rent seeking could present themselves. Others, such as the Private Finance Initiative (PFI), were arguably examples of rent seeking by political and business interest groups that aggravated the inefficiencies of the public sector. In some services, such as the NHS, the process of change in itself has arguably involved disruption and transition costs that have exceeded the potential benefits of the change. The lesson that should be learnt from the UK experience of public sector reform is that there is no obvious managerial or technical solution that can easily overcome the fundamental framework of incentives that prevails in a public service. The disciplines of the price mechanism and a hard budget constraint including bankruptcy are not available in the public sector. Moreover, resources are allocated in a political context where it is difficult to constrain demand and to control cost.

Cash limits and abandoning funny money

IN THE 1970S AND EARLY 1980S crude cash limits were imposed on government departments not so much to improve efficiency, but to ensure straightforward public expenditure control. There is no doubt that the decision to abandon the so-called Plowden public expenditure arrangements where public spending was planned over five years in volume terms so that no matter what happened to price inflation the same real level of public services would be provided represented a huge step towards public expenditure realism.

The failure of public sector reform

Not least because government departments had to account for what they were spending in real money rather than the 'funny money' of volume public expenditure planning expressed in constant prices.

The best account of the mess that public expenditure control got into on the 1970s and how cash limits returned the Treasury to reality remains Sir Leo Pliatzky's 'Getting and Spending: Public Expenditure, Employment and Inflation' (1982). Pliatzky was a career Treasury official and at the height of the fiscal crisis in 1976 he was the second permanent secretary in charge of public spending. Pliatzky was the quintessential Treasury knight and in retirement produced a readable and cogent account of what had gone wrong. Cash limits brought in some immediate control and also had the merits of abandoning the elaborate apparatus of the Plowden Public Expenditure Survey Committee (PESC) volume system. This change may have brought about greater control over total expenditure, but had little effect on efficiency, not that it was designed to explicitly to tackle efficiency. Although there was some evidence that the process of arbitrary cash limits themselves, concentrated the minds of spending departments, and may have extracted some efficiency gains, but these were incidental to their principal public expenditure control function.

The Financial Management Initiative

THE SERIOUS ATTEMPT to improve the efficiency of public spending as opposed to simply achieving better control over it was the value for money scrutiny process conducted by Sir Derek Rayner, the managing director from Marks & Spencer brought in by Mrs Thatcher. He established the Efficiency Unit in the Cabinet Office and later launched the Financial Management Initiative in 1982. Lord Rayner, as he became, had two broad approaches, short intense investigations of particular matters and broader lasting changes intended to alter the way government departments managed their resources. There was an emphasis on eliminating obsolete activities, terminating activities where the benefits were exceeded by the costs and simplifying administrative procedures. Rayner plainly had an impact and his process of scrutiny was much more effective than the Policy Analysis and Review system set up by Ted Heath, which Rayner had worked on in the early 1970s.

Rayner benefited from working for and reporting directly to the Prime Minister, Mrs Thatcher. A significant part of his acknowledged success was due to that. As David Heald comments in his book 'Public Expenditure: Its Defence and Reform' (1983), undoubted impact came from the Prime Minister's strong and direct support that ensured that ministers and civil servants had to co-operate with him. The Rayner approach was essentially narrow: using fewer inputs to achieve the same output. There was much less exploration of the kind of question that would concern a micro-economist about the public sector's efficiency. Yet as David Heald recognised, that deficiency should not lead one 'to dismiss the potential of Rayner's methodology for curbing X-inefficiency in the public sector', and many of the areas Rayner looked at involved management problems common to the private and public sector. Heald also shrewdly noted that much of Rayner's effectiveness could be attributed to the personal support of the Prime Minister, and it was not clear whether that effectiveness could be maintained once Lord Rayner returned to Marks & Spencer. In that sense the Rayner process was likely to be a one-off effort rather than a permanent institutional change.

There were many valuable suggestions about improvements in housekeeping, but the Rayner savings were principally of the 'saving the candle ends' variety and did little to improve the effectiveness of public expenditure. Where they probably had their main impact was when they recommended that something should stop or be cut back rather than identifying more efficient ways of doing things. The main impact of that was on official UK statistics, which were then principally the responsibility of the Central Statistical Office (CSO). Other scrutinies that attracted interest were the examination of the Ordnance Survey and the National Theatre Museum project.

Rayner's recommendations in relation to the CSO were highly contentious and may have had damaging consequences to the long-term efficiency of the public sector. The resources of the CSO were reduced and the range and focus of its work were narrowed. When the full effect of these changes were made many economists believed there was less reliable and less extensive information about the UK economy, which made the job of Treasury ministers managing public expenditure more difficult. Part of the explanation for the loose monetary policy in the late 1980s was the genuine belief among Treasury officials and ministers that the economy was not expanding as fast as it was and that there was more spare capacity to contain inflationary pressures than there really was. Interestingly enough, while Nigel Lawson, the Chancellor of the Exchequer involved, recognises the deficiency of the statistics that he was provided with, he does not blame the Rayner scrutiny of the CSO for their inadequacy.

Indeed, Lord Lawson admired the efficiency savings that the Rayner approach yielded and estimates that by 1986 the cumulative effective of the economies identified by Lord Rayner, along with a 20 percent reduction in the civil service payroll, amounted to some £1 billion. In the context of General Public Expenditure (excluding privatisation proceeds) of some £170 billion, it is clear, that the Financial Management Initiative and the Rayner scrutinies did not lead to a step change in public sector efficiency or a transformation of what the state was capable of doing effectively.

Lord Rayner was succeeded as head of the Prime Minister's Efficiency Unit by Robin Ibbs, who was recruited from ICI. He took the view that business management techniques could improve the performance of the public sector. His job was to try to get the public sector to mimic the behaviour of business. Shortly after I arrived in Whitehall, Sir Robin Ibbs was in turn succeeded by retired Civil Servant Sir Angus Frazer. I think it is fair to say that by that time,

1988, the FMI had lost most of its punch and the Prime Minister's annual Value for Money seminar at No 10 with individual departments and their Secretaries of State had become very much pro-forma affairs, if not part of what Walter Bagehot would have called the ceremonial side of government as opposed to the efficient part of it. That is not to say these seminars were not capable of stimulating a great deal of entertainment across Whitehall.

The Department of Employment had an extensive range of training and work programmes, which often involved working with the voluntary sector. These had been set up in some haste in the early and mid-1980s when unemployment was high and continuing to rise. It is not clear that they were as efficiently managed as they should have been and for several years the accounts of the department had been qualified. The Treasury was increasingly irritated by the Department and it is not surprising that in 1990 the Department of Employment had a very awkward Value for Money seminar with the Prime Minister.

The Department of Employment's latest project in 1990 was to create employer-led Training and Enterprise Councils, the TECs. The Prime Minister and her Policy Unit had been sceptical about the TECs from the beginning. No 10's concern was that instead of being bodies that local employers would get involved in and as a result start to spend more of their own company money on training, the TECs would become ineffective talking shops that would end up as business-led 'local soviets' to demand more government spending on training that employers should be paying for themselves. From the start the Value for Money Seminar was a difficult occasion, with the Prime Minister taxing everyone in the room from the Department, in her distinctive and penetrating manner. Things became more difficult when she turned her attention to TECs, asking what their purpose was. At that point the Department's Secretary unwisely thought it would be helpful to hand her a copy of the TECs' mission statement. Unfortunately this meant that from that point on the Prime Minister was the only person

The failure of public sector reform

in the room who had a copy of the mission statement and swiftly turned the situation to her advantage. She began by asking what was meant by the term 'mission statement'. She asked if they were planning a journey to Mars or some other part of outer space. In senior Whitehall terms the event had descended into chaos, if not Feydeau farce, with the Prime Minister able to run circles round everybody in the room, for her own amusement. When the meeting concluded at lunchtime, she reassured the recently appointed Secretary of State Michael Howard that this was none of his fault and she did not in any way hold him responsible, but instead turned on the Department's Secretary as he left and said 'please, no more programmes'. Within half an hour most of the private offices across Whitehall and certainly those in the Treasury were enjoying the Department of Employment's value for money disaster. Did it have any impact on policy or the operation of the TECs? None whatsoever.

The Audit Commission

ANOTHER BIG IDEA was the establishment of an audit commission to improve the efficiency and effectiveness of local authority expenditure. The Audit Commission was set up by Michael Heseltine in the early 1980s, because he did not believe that the old District Audit Service was up to the job. Heseltine wanted the skills of the private sector applied to local government to generate better value for money for the taxpayer. Local government had become a byword for expensive inefficiency in the 1970s. The reorganisation of local government in 1972 resulted in an increase in rate bills of over 30 per cent. The public reaction led to the setting up of Frank Layfield's inquiry into local authority finance. It was the background to the famous speech by Tony Crosland in 1976 announcing that the party in local authority spending was over.

The creation of the Audit Commission was resented by local authorities. It was perceived as an attempt by the Thatcher government to interfere in the autonomy of local councils and as an instrument for Maggie's cuts. From the start, the Audit Commission had a strong business and management consultancy imperative at its heart. The first Controller or chief executive, John Banham, was an experienced partner from McKinsey. Among its first officials was a secondee from the Treasury, an expert on operations analysis, who had once worked at the National Coal Board. The hallmark of the organisation became the publication of arresting reports identifying anomalies in local authority expenditure, looking at things such as the comparative cost of disposing of one ton of municipal refuse. In its first two years of operation it announced that it had identified over £1 billion of waste in local government. Following John Banham's departure to become Director General of the CBI, Howard Davies, another McKinsey man and Treasury official, continued in much the same vein. The biggest change or development was the Commission's growing confidence, reflected in the Commission owning up to the fact that in practice, it was commenting on 'policy,' rather than simply engaging in some kind of narrower audit.

By the early 1990s the mood was changing. The feeling inside the Commission and in Whitehall, was that the Commission was good at identifying what was wrong and how things could be improved. There was, however, no mechanism to translate the Commission's advice into improved efficiency. The Commission's reports and audits 'illuminated' as Howard Davies put it, but did not direct or in any way regulate. This began to change in the 1990s. The Conservative government made the Commission the inspector and effective policeman of Compulsory Competitive Tendering (CCT). This role went much further than traditional audit or illumination. The really big step to intrusive regulation came about as a result of John Major's innovation of the Citizen's Charter. The Audit Commission was given the job of applying the Citizen's Charter to local government.

One of the distinguishing features of the Audit Commission has

The failure of public sector reform

been mission creep. Having started on local councils, its core re-current work, it extended its interest into other areas of the public services where the statute establishing the Commission gave it a locus, such as the police. It was also invited by Conservative Health Ministers in the early 1990s to extend its scrutiny to the NHS. In many respects this mission creep was a tribute to the effectiveness of the Commission and the regard in which it came to be held in Whitehall. But these compliments and the extension of its role came at a price: the dilution of its original *raison d'être*. In short, it slowly moved from being an institution with a calculator and a sharp pencil that offered searching analysis and unpalatable home truths into being part of the treacle of public sector rhetoric. The once lucid analysis expressed in elegant English became the softly spoken syrup of public sector jabberwockery.

The desire to take an increased regulatory role in relation to lo-cal government chimed conveniently with the outlook of Labour Ministers in 1997. Before Labour took office the Controller of the Commission, a former social worker who had been Director of Social Services at Greenwich, had formulated a replacement for CCT with a broader and more qualitative approach to local serv-ices that became 'Best Value'. This turned into a disaster for local government in terms of performance. It involved the creation of an additional layer of inspectors on top of the District Audit Service. Best Value was followed by PIs and targets, and then by the Com-prehensive Performance Assessment. The Audit Commission ended up twenty years after its creation as a source of inefficiency in local government rather than an instrument for eradicating it.

Part of the explanation for this was the expansion of the role of the Commission and its extension into regulation. Yet part of it goes to the heart of the difficulty of obtaining value for money from the public sector. Michael Heseltine genuinely believed in private enterprise. He also believed in big government, and was comfortable with the 1970s corporate state that was the legacy of the Heath government. Heseltine, like Sir Robin Ibbs the head of

Mrs Thatcher's Efficiency Unit, also thought that business acumen harnessed to taxpayer's cash could deliver results. He believed that private sector practice could overcome the profound inefficiencies that result from a political market place and the absence of market disciplines like bankruptcy. Management skill and private sector techniques could overcome the inertia of the public service. He was later to apply this rubric to procurement at the Ministry of Defence.

When the Audit Commission operated with genuine flair the heart of its methodology was the application of OR (operations research) to local government spending. It was applying economic planning techniques perfected by organisations such as the National Coal Board to local government spending. It was interesting and provoking in its audacity, but bound to be disappointing in its practical results. Central planning does not work. The Commission's attempts to centrally engineer a step change in local authority efficiency were doomed to fail. It is in the tradition of the Soviet Gosplan, the Indian Licence Raj and the post-war Labour government's groundnut scheme. One size dreamt up in London cannot fit all, however clever the dreamers. One approach to social care and imposed on every local authority in England will not yield optimum results, because the process of discovery, experiment and failure is thwarted by bureaucratic central control. This applies every bit as much to Michael Heseltine's ambitions as it does to the targets imposed in recent years by Labour ministers.

English local government and health care presents a challenge. The principal decisions about funding, the extent of provision and preferred model for providing the principal public services such schools, hospitals and social care are decided in London. London decides on the details of public provision for 50 million of the UK's 60 million citizens. This is plainly impractical. It is a recipe for monolithic bureaucratic public services distinguished by low levels of productivity. Yet modifying it in a radical way is impossible without accepting two things: giving local government a powerful

The failure of public sector reform

and buoyant source of tax revenue; and abandoning the entrenched notion of a rough equality of public service provision in each local authority. There is a further practical difficulty: if local authorities were allowed to raise elastic revenue generating taxes such as income tax, there would still remain the problem of a highly dispersed regional tax base. Having the power to tax is one thing, having something to tax is another. Over the last forty years economic activity and the tax base has become increasingly concentrated in London and the South East of England.

A central feature of inefficiency in local authority expenditure in the UK is the complex framework of central government grants that fund around 75 per cent of councils' spending. For a hundred years public inquiry after public inquiry have concluded that there is a fundamental problem when the body that spends the money has no practical responsibility for raising money in taxes. In 1976 the Layfield report concluded that 'whoever is responsible for spending money should be responsible for raising it so that the amount of expenditure is subject to democratic control'. Layfield only repeated in less vivid tones what the Primrose Committee on Irish finance after Home Rule concluded in 1912 that 'a first principle of sound government is that the same authority that has the spending of revenue should have the burden and not infrequently the odium of raising that revenue' and that where one body does the taxing and another does the spending is 'a division of labour that leads to disaster.

To mark its first twenty-five years the Audit Commission appointed Duncan Campbell-Smith to write its official history. Campbell-Smith not only tells the story of the Audit Commission well – pulling no punches – but also provides a compelling account of the history of English local government since the 1980s in 'Follow the Money: The Audit Commission, Public Money and the Management of Public Services, 1983-2008' (2008). For many people there is nothing more boring than the words 'English local government', but there is nothing dull about Campbell-Smith's

Sorry, We Have No Money

account of it, because he has an eye for colour and vividly brings to life the personalities involved. They range from the cardigan-clad, pipe-smoking district auditors, who could happily pass half a morning re-selecting the English cricket team, to the Brechtian characters that led some Labour councils in the 1980s. Many, many things can be said about Dame Shirley Porter's tenure as Leader of Westminster City Council, but dull is not in the lexicon.

Campbell-Smith's book shows how the Audit Commission has lost its way and failed to deliver effective analysis of how public spending can be more efficiently spent. For any councillor wishing to understand the efficiency and effectiveness of their own authority the Annual Management Letter presented either by the District Auditor or by private auditors brought in to raise the game of the traditional district audit service is an unhelpful document. Broad generalities are expressed, the overall tone implies that across the country local authority services are improving in their value for money. When these letters are examined with any care the results of the exchanges are often at best feeble. What is worse, where councillors express concern about particular and specific difficulties such the council house rent accounts, knowing that there are genuine practical problems in their authority, far from assisting the councillors the authors of the management letters are more likely to retreat into unintelligible jargon. This is because they work closely with the local authority officers and they have no incentive to help councillors challenge the officers who advise them.

While the Audit Commission has presented steady progress in important public services and increased local authority efficiency, the ONS statisticians during the same period have exposed serious questions about efficiency and productivity that contradicts the Commission's core judgment. What is more, the principal areas of public expenditure that the ONS look at are precisely the same areas that the Audit Commission is charged with assessing, such as health, education and social services. Eric Pickles' decision as Secretary of State for Communities and Local Government to

The failure of public sector reform

announce the abolition of the Audit Commission in August 2010, reflects the Commission's disappointing performance. Nevertheless, Pickles did not hide his irritation about what he described as the Commission's champagne lifestyle or proposed salary for the new chief executive. When the appointment was about to be advertised the proposed salary was in excess of £200,000, suggesting that the organisation was oblivious to the stewardship of public resources during a fiscal crisis. The abolition of the Audit Commission represents the recognition that it had failed in its original purpose to improve public sector efficiency.

Contracting out and privatising services

IN THE 1980S AND 1990S local authorities and the National Health Service were under pressure to contract out and privatise as many services as possible, such as refuse collection, laundry, cleaning and catering. There were obvious and genuine benefits from doing much of this, but in truth it failed to deliver the efficiency and value for money benefits that had been hoped for. There were several reasons for this. The public sector is not consistently realistic in drawing up and managing contracts with the private sector. There were occasions when managers simply used contracts as a means of specifying a higher and more expensive level of service than went before. In principle these things can be dealt with simply by better contract management.

There are, however, more fundamental reasons why contracting out and privatising services has disappointed as a source of public sector efficiency. The principal reason for contracting out was that a private operator would be able to employ staff, particularly manual employees outside the terms of national public sector and local government pay bargaining. In many instances it may well have made sense in terms of quality, management control and convenience to directly employ the cleaners or caterers. While contracting out offers some scope to remedy a fundamentally defective set of arrangements, the core issue was public sector pay and conditions. Contracting out was fiddling at the edges, dressed up as fundamental reform.

The extent to which contracting out could yield benefits has been progressively undermined. The EU directive protecting employee rights when their employment changes, originally envisaged as protecting employees when a private sector firm is taken over by another such as the Kraft-Cadbury takeover, has been applied by the European Court of Justice to British public sector contracting. The Transfer of Undertakings Directive now means that when public sector workers are transferred to a bidder that wins the contract to provide a particular service, the public sector employees must continue to enjoy the same terms and conditions as they previously enjoyed in local government or the health service. This obviously blunts the effectiveness of contracting out. In 2004 Labour ministers agreed with the trade unions the so-called Warwick Agreement – it was negotiated at Warwick University – which took the Transfer of Undertakings (Protection of Employment) Regulations (TUPE) a stage further. If a former public sector worker is employed under a contracted-out arrangement and another private sector worker is employed and works beside them, the non-public sector worker has to be employed on the same terms and conditions as the former public sector worker who retains the expensive public sector terms and conditions. This effectively limits the benefits that contracting out could offer.

There are also genuine practical difficulties that relate to competition. It is hard to achieve effective savings when contracting out public services where there is little private sector competition to manage those services. In refuse collection and waste management, local authorities are confronted by a limited number of private sector providers that amount to monopoly suppliers of service.

Government agencies

TOWARDS THE END of Margaret Thatcher's long period of office she was persuaded by the head of her Efficiency Unit, Sir Robin Ibbs, that one way to achieve greater efficiency in public expenditure would be to create executive agencies run as businesses at arm's length from government departments and away from direct day-to-day ministerial management. This was set out in a paper 'Improving Management in Government - The Next Steps' (1988). The principal official who carried them out was Sir Peter Kemp, a former Treasury official and trained accountant originally from the private sector, working at the Cabinet Office. The idea was that a professional manager using modern business methods would lead to more efficient public expenditure. There was no doubt about the enthusiasm of many senior officials about the concept of arms' length agencies.

The idea that simply separating ministers from the day-to-day management of the details of programme administration would deliver a step change in efficiency was, however, naive. Setting up a government agency does not overcome the inherent reasons why public sectors experience problems with efficiency:

- No use of the price mechanism;
- No hard budgets;
- No bankruptcy; and
- Producer interests engaging in rent seeking.

No amount of professional administration, business rhetoric or management consultancy can overcome those fundamental constraints that relate to resource allocation through the public sector and its political processes. Of course, for senior civil servants working at the Training Agency or the Health and Safety Executive the idea of working without day-to-day supervision by ministers was a very attractive one, although whether zealousness to achieve full public sector efficiency was at the heart of every senior official who extolled its potential merits is another matter.

Sorry, We Have No Money

Twenty years later there is no evidence that any of these agencies have delivered consistent efficiency gains. In the UK the notion of removing public sector programmes from day-to-day ministerial interference and ad hoc priorities was an understandable and respectable proposition. Yet it was a naive one. Leaving aside the fundamental question of the efficiency of resources allocation outside of the price mechanism, it is not clear in practice how public sector bodies can operate without overall ministerial oversight, given that ministers are ultimately accountable to Parliament and now – being realistic – to the 24-hour media. There is nothing new in this practical difficulty. Bagehot in his book 'The English Constitution' explained why early 19th century welfare reform that was intended to save money and increase efficiency foundered on the problem of the Poor Law Commission's accountability to Parliament. Although some other countries such as Canada and the US also experimented with the establishment of executive agencies it is not at all clear that theses bodies resulted in the step change in efficiency that either Sir Robin Ibbs or Sir Peter Kemp promised Mrs Thatcher. There are accounts and boards of directors but the ultimate sanction of financial failure cannot exist in a non-market setting.

The creation of what became known as the 'next step agencies' substantially narrowed effective ministerial responsibility. For several decades government ministers slowly and incrementally sidestepped the traditional doctrine that ministers were responsible for all the actions of their departments and officials. This was a train that had been in motion for a long time, but the creation of the executive agencies was a decisive point in the effective narrowing of ministerial responsibility. Whether its narrowing has increased either the effectiveness or efficiency of the public service is not clear. The crucial issue at the heart of the public service efficiency challenge is a lack of discipline, there is no threat of private sector bankruptcy. In the absence of that financial discipline, elaborate frameworks of political accountability have been erected. In Britain

The failure of public sector reform

the principal form that it took was ministerial accountability; without it, it is not all clear who is ultimately accountable for a service. The ministers are responsible for the policy and the agencies for carrying it out. Yet the interaction between policy and execution is so complex that their neat separation is often close to impossible. What is plain is that the salaries and compensation packages of many senior managers have mimicked the behaviour of the private sector.

Shadow prices, internal markets and purchaser provider splits

IN 1988, TOWARDS THE END OF THE THATCHER ADMINISTRATION, the government's record on the health service came under intense pressure. Despite having increased public spending on health significantly in real terms and making increasing use of devices such as contracting out there was a growing feeling that more should be done to the health service to improve it so that taxpayers got better value from the service and patients had greater choice and satisfaction. This resulted in a radical analysis of the organisation and structure of the NHS. The review started from the position that health care should be free at the point of use, but made significant changes to the way the health services were planned and organised to improve them. The Bevan model introduced in 1948 is unusual among OECD countries. It is essentially a nationally planned health service analogous to the command economies that socialist economies had for the production of all goods and services. Aneurin Bevan in his book 'In Place of Fear' described the free health service as 'pure Socialism'. In one sense the system was efficient, its command and control structure enabled the Treasury to hold down spending on the NHS. The result was that the UK spent less as a proportion of national income on health care than many OECD countries, and roughly half that of the US, yet had comparable health outcomes in terms of morbidity and mortality.

The result of the review was the 1989 White Paper 'Working for Patients' and the creation of an internal market inside the NHS. It would enable the NHS to achieve efficiencies by obtaining greater information about its routine costs, the creation of a regime of shadow prices which would enable health service managers to shop around within the health service to get the best results for the cash allocated to them. There was a division between the health service managers who commission services for patients and the parts of the health service that provide the service, and the commissioners were obliged to shop around for the best internal price for an operation or procedure.

In many ways it is a very attractive and persuasive model. In principle it gave patients genuine choice about where they could have an operation, although in practice when they tried to make use of that freedom it turned out often to be a chimera. The Treasury's first reflex was to oppose it for no better grounds than the fact that exposing the costs and prices of the health internal market may actually increase the pressure to spend money on it. The Treasury was also mindful that the NHS with its command and control framework of socialist planning was an extremely effective mechanism for controlling spending on health care, particularly compared to other countries that used public-private hybrid insurance arrangements. These reservations simply reflected the Treasury's customary interest in departmental expenditure control rather than any sophisticated analysis of value for money and effectiveness of public expenditure.

Some individual members of the Government Economic Service expressed privately more interesting and fundamental reservations about whether the NHS internal market could achieve its ostensible objectives. In summary, their concern was the classic statement of the way 'shadow' prices cannot deliver real efficiency, because they are essentially artificially derived, and the institutions setting

The failure of public sector reform

them and paying them are not subject to the full discipline of the market and ultimately with bankruptcy. As it happened, at the time that the British NHS was experimenting with internal markets and shadow prices as a reform of its own command socialist planned health care system, Mikhail Gorbachev was introducing similar reforms to the whole of the Soviet economy. These British government economists, as well as doubting whether the internal market would yield the hoped-for benefits here, also wondered whether the Gorbachev reforms in the USSR might shock the moribund system into non-performance, if not full crisis, without yielding clear benefits, making the whole system less manageable. In the UK the system involved a huge upheaval, vast administrative costs, expensive-to-obtain information about the prices and a great deal of management distraction. Its obvious benefits were less clear, although many health care professionals continued to be attracted to it and supportive of it.

In 1997 one of the first actions of the New Labour government was to fulfil its pledge to scrap the NHS's internal market. There is no doubt that this was a symbolically popular move among many doctors, nurses and managers as well as the trade unions. There were other managers who saw it as not much more than yet another health management reorganisation being made with the added cost of losing some information and useful flexibility. What is interesting is that by the end of its first term Labour was beginning to return to many of the devices of the internal market and much of New Labour's public services reform agenda was essentially a version of the internal market in health that had been abolished to such acclaim. By the time Tony Blair left office in 2007 the internal market with its purchaser-provider split, 'book and choose' and free-standing independent foundation trust hospitals was back in all but name and if anything taken a stage further. Yet there is no clear evidence that in its new guise shadow pricing and independent providers have delivered efficiently. The ONS picture is clear there has been no dramatic improvement in efficiency and most of the

Sorry, We Have No Money

increased activity has simply reflected additional cash resources. UK health spending is now much closer to the European average than it was. The clear evidence that the NHS is efficient in the sense of achieving the same as other countries, that use noticeably more resources, has gone. Moreover, no health services structure could compensate for nationally agreed pay for hospital consultants and primary care doctors that in short paid them much more to do less. Aneurin Bevan boasted that he persuaded the elite cadre of hospital doctors – what we now know as consultants – to work in the health service by 'filling their mouths with gold.' His New Labour successors took this a stage further by filling every doctor's mouth with gold, not just the elite grade of specialist hospital doctors, but general practitioners as well. No arrangements could deliver efficiency, effectiveness or value for money in the face of that approach to public sector pay.

The Citizen's Charter

THE NEXT BIG IDEA in British public service reform was the Citizen's Charter. John Major formulated it as a way of giving citizens practical rights over the services that the state provides for them. In many respects it was an attractive idea about empowering individuals against large impervious public sector bureaucracies. There was no doubt that John Major's interest in establishing the Citizen's Charter was genuinely motivated by his own concern about the way people experienced public services, not least their perception of being patronised and being given a service on sufferance rather than 'as of right'. Providing the public with effective rights in the sense of effective remedies when their rights under a charter were breached was in practice much harder to accomplish than the process of public iteration and announcement of the rights in such a charter. In the context of the British public sector the central problem was that a right with an effective remedy would normally mean that an already inefficient service would simply demand more public money to fulfil its duties under the Citizen's Charter. The Treasury for that reason was viscerally opposed to it and in practice the detailed rights and remedies set out under the framework of the charter were very carefully circumscribed so that it had little practical effect. The Citizen's Charter was an interesting and an attractive idea, but it never could overcome the fundamental problems that emerged when it was first looked into by Treasury officials, with the result it never really took off despite the Prime Minister's genuine interest in it.

The private finance initiative

JOHN MAJOR, BOTH AS CHANCELLOR AND PRIME MINISTER, was interested in involving the private sector in financing and improving the management of public sector investment. From the early 1980s public sector investments had been subjected to strict tests to assess their rate of return. In the 1981 these tests were summarised in the so-called Ryrie Rules named after their author Sir John Ryrie, the Treasury official who chaired the committee that constructed them. They were formulated in 1981 when the UK had a significant nationalised industry sector and have to be understood in that context. The public sector can borrow relatively cheaply in the gilt market and that can lead to an over-accumulation of public sector capital that cannot be justified in terms of its social or economic returns. This was plain from the nationalised industries themselves, which in the 1970s absorbed around 20 per cent of UK fixed capital investment and accounted for about 15 per cent of employment yet only produced around 10 per cent of GDP. The principal recommendation of the committee was that to guard against such an over-accumulation of capital a special discount factor of 6 per cent should be applied to public sector investment. In practice the rules presented a significant obstacle in the way of government departments engaging in capital projects unless they could be demonstrated to offer value for money on quite a strict test.

Sorry, We Have No Money

It should be noted that the rules, apart from the specific issues involved, were formulated against a particular policy background. The first was the priority given in the periods between 1975 and 1986 to controlling public spending in general and capital spending in particular to reduce government expenditure and borrowing, given the impact that the PSBR had on the counterparties that made up the broad money supply, M3. There was also was a recognition on the part of the Treasury and Conservative Ministers such as Sir Geoffrey Howe, Jock Bruce-Gardyne and Layfield that in the 1960s and early 1970s governments had been too willing to spend money on wasteful infrastructure projects and other investment that did not stand up to proper scrutiny and turned out to be white elephants. Indeed Nigel Lawson and Jock Bruce-Gardyne had written a book about it called 'The Power Game: An examination of decision-making in Government' (1976). The most notorious example of this was the Humber Bridge project. This was announced by the Minister of Transport, Barbara Castle, to try to save a safe Labour seat in a difficult by-election in Hull in 1966. The financial consequences of this continued to cause problems for the Treasury right up until the 1990s.

The Ryrie rules were much maligned. They became a sort of Treasury bogeyman which lobby groups both inside government spending departments and outside blamed for every disappointment they received. The detail of the rules may have been slightly too tightly drawn, but their fundamental purpose was to prevent a repeat of the sort of episode exemplified by the Humber Bridge. There is no doubt that they were frustrating to ministers and a whole range of government departments. They also effectively frustrated business lobby groups that had an interest in public sector investment, or to be more precise a vested interest in the contracts they could receive from being paid to construct the roads and bridges and so on that would be involved. These vested interests were opposed to legitimate public policy interests in, say, suitable transport connections for their employees and suppliers, which is

The failure of public sector reform

part of the general interest and debate about the provision of public infrastructure.

In the second half of the 1980s these business interests, often from the construction and civil engineering industries, mounted a sustained lobby against the strictures of the Ryrie rules. In order to get around the matter of capital spending representing public expenditure and needing to be financed by government borrowing, these business lobbies argued that they could pay for the construction themselves. They would use their own balance sheets to borrow to pay for the construction and the public sector could lease back the building or road, paying some sort of user fee or annual charge. It was an attractive proposition. Government ministers got their chosen capital projects and firms got the contracts to build and manage them.

There was from the start a fundamental flaw in these attractive propositions. The British government can borrow more cheaply than any private sector borrower. This means that, however the arrangements are structured, the financing in the long term would turn out to be more expensive than the taxpayer footing the bill in the normal way. And if borrowing is needed nothing is cheaper for the British government than the gilt market. The British government can always mobilise huge sums of money for public spending and complex investment projects more cheaply than private sector investors. The Treasury does this through general taxation and its capacity to borrow in the gilt market. It is, moreover, something that has been demonstrated from the time of the original creation of the Bank of England and funded national debt in 1694, through to the Napoleonic Wars and the financing of the two world wars in the 20th century.

The decision to go ahead with the Channel Tunnel, which was intended to be privately financed without any public finance, was a fillip to the private finance lobby. Given the huge time and cost overruns on many large public sector infrastructure projects from hospitals to roads, a further argument was developed to support the

Sorry, We Have No Money

private finance initiative. This was that the private sector is so efficient it could manage these complex projects much better than the private sector and yield efficiency savings so great that they would more than compensate for the additional cost of private finance making these schemes. There is no doubt that this had a nugget of respectability; the inefficiency of public sector procurement and infrastructure investment was a serious matter. The suggestion of transferring the genuine risk and associated costs of such projects to the private sector was an interesting and worthwhile proposition to explore.

On robust examination, however, the arguments in favour of the PFI never stood up. I worked at the Treasury when it was first explored by John Major's government. It was plain to me that it could not deliver what it was cracked up to offer. It was supposed to give the taxpayer investment projects - from schools to railways - more efficiently managed and at a lower cost, compared with normally financed government investment. This was always implausible. As well as the crude business and political vested interests in play, the PFI in the 1990s at a glance played well in relation to other less venal parts of the broader public policy agenda. On the face of it the PFI was consistent with the notion of making the public sector more efficient by bringing in the private sector. It ideologically appeared to fit consistently with contracting and privatisation. It was seen as bringing in private sector disciplines where the activities themselves could not be privatised.

The PFI also fitted neatly into what might be called the New Zealand public sector reform agenda. In the 1980s a Labour government in New Zealand embarked on a radical market-oriented economic and public sector reform programme. It was driven forward by the Finance Minister, Sir Roger Douglas. By the 1990s a cross-party consensus in New Zealand had embarked on such a comprehensive range of public service change and employed the price mechanism in so many different ways that the country became the benchmark of effective policy making. 'New Zealand's new public management' became the model that much of the world including the UK and US looked to. Its agenda is probably most concisely summarised by in a Brookings Institution paper written by Donald Kettl entitled 'The Global Public Management Revolution' (2000). Among these reforms was the introduction of accruals accounting, combined with ensuring that the public sector properly looked after the assets on its balance sheet. One of the criticisms of the public sector was that it allowed its capital assets to depreciate through poor maintenance in a way the private sector would not. The PFI structure played very well in the context of that debate. The contracts would specify annual maintenance, and government departments when making contracts would have to fess up to the full depreciation cost of the investment they were embarking on. There is no doubt that the PFI was worked up to fit the zeitgeist of the period.

After the 1992 election the Major government in the 'Autumn Statement' went ahead with the PFI, overriding the traditional Treasury reservations about it. The much-loathed Ryrie rules themselves had in fact been replaced in the spring of 1989. Relatively few projects, however, went ahead, because the Treasury rightly retained rules about there being a genuine transfer of risk between the public and private contractor, which in practice vitiated many proposals. Even so, by 1996 there were enough PFI projects in play to enable the economists from Goldman Sachs to express concern at the time of Kenneth Clarke's final Conservative Budget about the extent of the government's off-balance sheet private finance liabilities.

After 1997 that test concerning risk transfer to the private sector was further relaxed, if not completely abandoned, and the specific rules about PFI contracts genuinely transferring risk to the private sector went. The purpose of these changes was to enable as much PFI-financed investment to take place as possible because it was a way of obtaining off-balance sheet capital spending that was neither fully scored for government expenditure nor for public

Sorry, We Have No Money

borrowing. This new iteration of the PFI rules also neatly fitted into the modified New Labour zeitgeist: it was a private sector solution, it appealed to vested business interests and it fitted with a new framework of national accounts accounting. In 1998 the Treasury announced a new framework of national public sector accounting that contributed to changing the presentation of government borrowing to separate out borrowing to finance capital investment from borrowing to finance current consumption spending. This new presentation of the public accounts was to facilitate Gordon Brown's much-trumpeted fiscal rules. These were that the government should only borrow for investment and over the economic cycle the stock of government debt should be set at a stable and prudent level in relation to national income – 40 per cent was the chosen ratio of GDP. These rules were dressed up as strict, but on any careful examination were plainly elastic. Such things as how tightly do you define investment and what constitutes the economic cycle obviously offer the Treasury huge scope in financial casuistry, normally to claim that they have met such rules. The PFI, however, was an additional convenience in obtaining public investment outside the rules that relate to government borrowing even if in the end it turns out to be more expensive.

The remarkably effective lobbying of many business interests under John Major had unlocked the door to the PFI, but the transfer of risk rules until 1997 had meant that the scale of the programme was relatively modest. Under New Labour, however, there was a flood of PFI projects. As interest rates fell PFI projects were refinanced, but the taxpayer continued to be locked into contracts at the old rate of interest. After the millennium and the stock market 'tech wreck' many traditional construction and engineering companies marketed themselves to investors and fund managers as not 'boring old-fashioned construction firms', but exciting sexy 'private finance firms' with 'secure and lucrative' public sector contracts.

These contracts have turned out to be much more expensive for the taxpayer than normal public expenditure. They have not obviously reduced all the normal procurement risks in the way that had been alleged. And they may have contributed to making public expenditure less efficient because of their inflexibilities and the perverse incentives that they create. Moreover, a flood of capital investment in, for example, school laboratories, hospital operating facilities and university libraries will not yield expected benefits without adequate current or revenue expenditure to provide for their day-to-day use and services. An increase in school physics laboratories is of little use without a matching increase in suitably trained science teachers. There have also been a host of complaints about the quality of the buildings and their availability in the evening or at weekends. A private contractor has no incentive to make a facility available to the wider community if it is outside their contract. Where facilities such as bridges have been constructed there are also a wide range of complex issues surrounding user charges and ensuring that a monopoly position is not exploited by the firm providing the facility. There is no clear evidence that the PFI has provided a step change in public sector efficiency any more than the other innovations that have been tried.

In many respects, as Mayor of London Ken Livingstone was the sort of politician who exemplified what went wrong with public spending after 1998. As he jokingly, although provocatively told one Greater London Authority Assembly member 'Remember, I am a tax-and-spender.' That was reflected in both the threefold increase in the budgets that the Mayor presented and the council tax precept for which he was responsible rising over two and a half times. Yet Ken Livingstone got one thing right as Mayor of London. He was against Gordon Brown's decision to pay for the modernisation of the London Underground through the Treasury's creation of a hybrid public private partnership (PPP). The collapse of Metronet is an illustration of the broader concerns about value for money in the PFI.

The Treasury was determined that the modernisation would be financed off the government's balance sheet through the private

Sorry, We Have No Money

finance framework. Given the risks involved, private investors would not accept the transfer of these risks, so a conventional PFI arrangement could not be established. Instead a complicated hybrid PPP was established. A consortium of companies came together in a specially set up company called Metronet. Along with Tube Lines, Metronet was awarded a thirty-year contract to reverse decades of neglected capital investment in London Underground's rail infrastructure. The Public Accounts Committee report, 'The Department for Transport: The failure of Metronet' (2010) explains what happened. The taxpayer lost between £170 million and £410 million as a result of Metronet's poor financial control and inadequate corporate governance. The report describes the Department of Transport's assumption that Metronet would put in place robust financial management controls and strong corporate governance arrangements as 'naive' and unsurprisingly 'did not hold'. Transport for London and the Mayor London could not exercise effective oversight of the arrangement because they could not obtain the information needed to oversee the contract. The arbitration arrangements were flawed because the Arbiter could only get involved if invited to do so by all the parties involved. The Department had no right of access to the Arbiter and could not direct him to carry out an investigation. The Department for Transport failed to plan for the additional risks arising out of Metronet's 'tied supply' chain. In this extraordinary arrangement, Metronet's suppliers were its own shareholders. Each of the companies invested £30 million of equity and £40 million of debt into Metronet. The Department of Transport assumed that Metronet would have a firm grip on its suppliers. There was, however, a 'conflict of interests caused by Metronet's shareholders being its main suppliers'. The owners of Metronet instead had little interest in establishing effective controls to ensure that it made a return on its PPP contract, given that as suppliers they would make money by working for it. This meant that there was little incentive to control costs. In 2007 the cost of refurbishing each of the Tube stations that Metronet worked on was twice the estimated cost in the budget. The Department of Transport also assumed that Metronet's bankers would exercise strong financial oversight of Metronet's business operations. In fact, they successfully reduced their own risk before they signed the PPP contracts by obtaining a guarantee that London Underground would meet 95 per cent of Metronet's borrowing in the event of a default. Metronet's lenders then reduced their risk further by obtaining a letter of comfort from the Department of Transport that it would fund the 95 per cent guarantee if London Underground could not do so. The Department of Transport was therefore very naive to expect institutions lending money to Metronet to exert strong financial oversight of it when the taxpayer had taken on all but 5 per cent of the lenders' risk. The Public Accounts committee concluded that it was 'appalled by the cavalier attitude to protecting public money that the Department displayed by claiming that its decision to use Metronet contracts had been vindicated because there would have been an even greater loss had the upgrades been overseen by London Underground'. Moreover, the Department for Transport had ignored recommendations made by the National Audit Office in 2004 to avoid a hands-off approach to overseeing the upgrading of the London underground railway.

Only someone who believed in the tooth fairy could have imagined that the PFI could offer both genuine value for money and the real transfer of risk from the taxpayer to private sector. But there were many politicians and businessmen and women who found it convenient to believe in fairy tales when it came to the PFI. For politicians its attraction was straightforward. It enabled them to announce spending today that would neither have to be paid for until tomorrow nor breach their framework of fiscal rules. For politicians it had all the attraction of the Enron factor: off-balance sheet accounting. For business, it meant lucrative government contracts ultimately paid for by the taxpayer and huge scope to manipulate the financial arrangements of the projects for the benefit of their shareholders. The scope for this has been so great that traditional construction companies have rebranded themselves to their investors as 'sexy and exciting' service companies generating predictable, recurring revenues from PFI contracts. The only surprise in all this has been the way the Treasury and Gordon Brown embraced it. Traditionally, the Treasury under all previous governments has been the Praetorian Guard protecting the taxpayer. Yet over the PFI in general and the PPP for the Tube, the Treasury sold the long-term interests of the taxpayer down the river.

The lesson from this saga is that there are some risks that only the taxpayer and the public sector can sensibly take on. They cannot ever be effectively transferred to the private sector at a reasonable cost. These big infrastructure projects need to be funded by the state. The issue should not be how could the Treasury get them financed by the private sector, off-balance sheet, at greater longer-terms cost. Instead, the question should be whether the project is justified on a rigorous and robust application of full cost benefit analysis.

London as a regional economy is in an odd position. It is by any international standard an economic powerhouse. London desperately needs a huge improvement in its rail transport infrastructure. Projects such as Crossrail and the Chelsea–Hackney line would yield huge economic and social benefits. They would expand the economic and tax base not just of London, but also of Britain as a whole. Yet the government will not finance them properly. This reluctance to do what only the government can do in London, when by any normally rigorous standard the projects should go ahead, leads to bizarre results.

The most obvious is delay. If death came from the same division in the Treasury that decided investment in London's transport, we would all live a long time. But delay is just the start. The refusal to invest taxpayers' money properly leads to the creation of overly cumbersome and complicated specialist private sector financing vehicles. The object lesson here is the Tube modernisation programme and Metronet. The worst consequence is that PFI

The failure of public sector reform

funding inflates the cost and that inflated cost can only be recouped from the fare-paying public, which is why travelling even with an Oyster Card in London is so expensive. The way that Crossrail will be financed illustrates the core problem that arises when governments try to finance complex high-risk but necessary infrastructure investment through the private sector. It is plain that the lion's share of the money will come from private investors. The danger of this is that the only way that it gets paid for is by a 'premium' fare structure, like the Heathrow to Paddington and the Liverpool Street to Stanstead services. That would greatly reduce its value to Londoners and the wider economic and social benefits that it should generate. London has an entrenched unemployment problem. The cost of getting to work is part of it. A premium rail service would do little to tackle it. London needs investment funded by the taxpayer. The lessons of PFI and Metronet's collapse are that in the long run, investment funded by the taxpayer saves money and in London would generate a stronger economic and tax base for Britain as a whole.

Public sector investment is most cheaply financed by the government itself through its power to tax and capacity to borrow. Off-balance sheet public expenditure is in the long run more expensive and its clumsy and perverse incentives can actually result in less efficient public expenditure. Moreover, the private finance does not offer any kind of silver bullet to increase public expenditure efficiency. If anything it is part of the potential fundamental government failure that mirrors the notion of market failure of allocating resources through bureaucratic and political mechanisms rather than the price mechanism. In that sense, PFI as an attempt to 'reform' the public sector and achieve a step change in performance is another disappointment, albeit an unusually expensive and in that sense an egregious public sector reform failure.

In many respects the principal lesson to be drawn from the PFI episode and the Metronet saga in particular is that in terms of large and complex infrastructure projects it is almost always the state that will have to take on the burden of the risk. These risks are too great to be transferred to the private sector at reasonable cost. Moreover, it is not clear that these risks can ever in practice be completely transferred because the political and public interest is so great that if the private sector were to step away the public sector would have to step in. Where such risks are transferred, leaving aside the direct long-term public sector costs to the taxpayer, there are in many cases other equally burdensome costs that relate to user charges, pricing and completion policy. The state has to recognise that it will have to construct and acquire expensive capital assets. That cannot be evaded. In terms of their long-term cost and efficient management that will normally mean they have to be bought, paid for and controlled by the public sector in the normal way. That means that public sector capital investment projects have to be rigorously assessed to ensure that they will earn an appropriate rate of return. And that capital investment and any borrowing that may attach to it have to be scored on the government's balance sheet as government spending and borrowing. The practice of employing the PFI to avoid placing that spending and borrowing on the public sector balance sheet should ended. That does not mean that in no circumstances can there ever be any use of the private sector in public sector procurement or financing of public sector investment. Nor does it mean that there are no circumstances where private finance cannot be used. Rather, such investment should be subjected to proper scrutiny and assessment and there should not be an off-balance sheet bogus accounting incentive for public investment to be carried out through the private sector as a mechanism for avoiding the rigorous assessment that should take place. This means abandoning the PFI as it has been used in the UK. That would represent a step to realism about the costs, burdens and efficiency of public sector capital spending.

That would involve a significant reordering of public expenditure priorities. There are now some 800 PFI projects, amounting to £65 billion. The House of Lords Committee on Economic Affairs in its report on the PFI has recommended that estimates of the total level of off-balance sheet public sector liabilities be published alongside statistics for the level of public sector debt.

New Labour's public service reform agenda

As PUBLIC SPENDING ROSE after 1998, and particularly after 2000, Labour ministers became increasingly concerned about getting demonstrable results for the higher levels of spending. There were a succession of policy initiatives that had been more or less tried by the Conservatives in the 1980s and 1990s to ensure that money followed patients and pupils. Extensive use was made of targets and Local Area Agreements were introduced that offered additional resources for specific objectives. In the NHS, payment by results was introduced; for schools, a pupil-based funding formula was developed, and the use of quasi markets was explored to stimulate the more efficient use of public money. The watch-words of Labour's public reform agenda were 'contestability' and 'money following the client'. Professor Tony Travers expressed the position concisely, writing in *Public Finance* in 2006 that 'simply pushing additional cash into hospitals and schools has, at best, produced debatable results. The lack of trusted productivity measures means that there is no real way of knowing how well the extra post-2000 resources have been spent'. In a sense, Labour's huge increases in public spending combined with their public service agreements and targets could be seen as a distinct public sector reform agenda in its own right. The overall approach in England was to create a highly centralised set of public services delivered though detailed national policy guidance, elaborate targets, specific grants and policy inspection regimes.

Central government departments do not develop and plan policies in a cost-effective manner that represents value for money. The Public Accounts Committee in 2008 examined financial and resource management across Whitehall departments that spend a total of some £670 billion. Managing financial resources to deliver better public services showed that 'few departmental boards are presented with accurate, timely and integrated financial and operational performance information'. Departments do not have the information to make well-informed decisions on use of resources and the financial implications of their policies. Only 41 per cent of government departments' policy proposals included a full financial appraisal and only 20 per cent of policy decisions were based on a thorough assessment of their financial implications. Under-spending of budgets often reflected unnecessary levels of contingency that prevented resources from being used on higher priority programmes, rather than good financial management where it reflects a decision to carry forward efficiency savings. The forecasting and monitoring of in-year expenditure is not consistent with actual expenditure incurred and often varies significantly from forecasts produced a few months before. The report concluded that departments do not have 'reliable information on the unit costs of key outputs to gauge whether costs are reasonable and commensurate with quality of service delivered'.

The British public sector has been subjected to a whole range of attempts to make it more efficient, effective and responsive. Most of the initiatives, from Lord Rayner's scrutinies to contracting out and the creation of the Audit Commission, have been worthwhile and interesting exercises to try to improve the work of the public sector. Some, such as cash limits, the Rayner scrutiny process and contracting out, improved financial control and genuinely rooted out examples of public sector X-inefficiency. Yet overall they have not resulted in a sustained institutional dynamic that has produced an obvious improvement in the public sector's efficiency. This is partly because some of the reforms simply modified the framework in which the precise manner of such losses of X-efficiency takes place. A good example of this is contracting out, where contracts can be over-specified and commissioned in a manner that is careless on value for money. Moreover, contracting out often only served

The failure of public sector reform

an effective purpose by enabling an organisation such as a local authority to get around expensive, efficient and entrenched public sector producer interest groups. Directly employed public sector workers whose expensive terms and conditions are nationally agreed, meant that it often made sense in terms of cost to contract out, although it often resulted in less effective management control over the service. The more obvious thing to do would be to tackle those entrenched public sector costs directly.

Continuous change has become a feature of UK public sector management since the 1970s. Moira Gibb, the Chief Executive of the London Borough of Camden coined the aphorism 'the only constant, is change itself' when she worked as the Director of Housing and Social Services in the Royal Borough of Kensington and Chelsea in the late 1990s. Many effective public sector managers believe that this process of permanent change in much of public policy making has been inconsistent with sensible management. Constant change obstructs competent management in a fruitless ambition for transformation. The British public sector was no more able to use efficiently a significant increase in resources in the 2000s than it was in the 1970s. That suggests that despite the extensive range of public sector management reform that has been tried, none of it has come anywhere near to overcoming the fundamental obstacles to public service efficiency, which are rooted in the political and bureaucratic market place, and a lack of effective incentives to control costs. It is therefore important to be realistic about the limitations of what can be achieved as a result of better public sector management. Searching for sustained improvements in the efficiency of public sector spending is in many respects a chimera. That means in assessing what the state is going do, and how extensive its intervention will be. The potential benefits and cost of the spending involved have to be rigorously assessed. It also requires the making of genuine choices and recognising the issue of affordability. Importantly, it implies that governments should avoid the conceit that they can achieve significant ambitions simply by spending money more efficiently. Moreover, people should not be misled into believing that a managerial agenda, whether it is accruals accounting, next step agencies or management consultancy and borrowing from the private sector, can overcome the inherent obstacles that limit and blunt the performance of the public sector.

Chapter 7: Britain's regional problem: the caring hand that cripples?

SINCE THE SLUMP OF THE 1920S and the first stages of the decline of the manufacturing industries created during the industrial revolution, Britain has had a regional economic problem. The traditional industries of the first industrial nation were concentrated in the north of England, Scotland and Wales. The economic activity that replaced them tended to be located in the south and east of England, whether these activities were the light electrical manufacturing of the 1930s or the financial and other services developed in the 1980s and 1990s. This shift in economic activity would probably have had a decisive effect under any circumstances, but it was overlaid by a further protracted change in the location of economic activity. The end of empire, imperial preference and the dislocations in trade generated by the two world wars shifted economic activity from the Commonwealth to trade with continental Europe. This process was given greater and decisive impetus by membership of the EEC in 1973, which further shifted trade and economic activity to the southeast of England.

Britain's long relative economic decline that became increasingly apparent in the 1950s and 1960s and threatened to become an absolute decline in the 1970s was a complex phenomenon with many dimensions to it. These ranged from the disadvantages that arose from being the first industrial nation to much wider social and political matters. Among them are the issues of:

❑ Management competence;

❑ Arguments about entrepreneurial dynamism and the social status of capitalists; and

❑ The costs that arose out of Britain's residuary international role as a former imperial power and specifically the amount spent on defence.

Many of these discussions go far beyond what it is possible for governments to change by policy such as those contained in Martin Wiener's 'English Culture and the Decline of the Industrial Spirit', even if they are true. And it should be recognised that this so-called declinist literature associated with Martin Wiener and

Britain's regional problem

Correlli Barnett's 'The Audit of War' (1987) has been subject to extensive challenge. The gist of the Wiener thesis was that successful businessmen once they had made their money would buy country estates, attempt to acquire aristocratic titles and their sons would deliberately avoiding working in industry as a means of confirming the family's new status. Barnett has a similar but more technocrat approach. He argues that there was a tendency for generalists rather than technical experts to achieve status and decision-making positions, that in particular public schools emphasised the study of the classics over that of the sciences. The most comprehensive challenge to these arguments has come from W D Rubinstein's 'Capitalism, Culture and Decline in Britain, 1750-1990' (1993), the nub of his argument being that while business elites were often keen to take on the status of nobility, in Britain they were no more prone to this than in other countries and if anything at the end of the 19th century more titles of aristocracy were granted to businessmen in countries such as Austria-Hungary and Prussia than in Britain. Therefore to locate any relative decline in British economic performance principally in these 'socialite' analyses is probably misplaced. Interestingly, Lord Roll in his book 'Where did we go wrong?' (1995) dismissed these sort of arguments that he called 'gentrification theory', saying that these 'survivals' – Ascot, Henley and morning coats – 'count for as much or as little as the obligatory dinner jackets at the Brenner Park Hotel in Baden-Baden, the splendid jewellery worn by the multitudes of German ladies at the Salzburg Festival'. It is interesting that Roll should take this view, given that he was born and brought up in Habsburg Vienna and plainly knew a 'Finance Baron' when he saw one. Roll also makes the interesting point that it was an American economist, Thorstein Veblen, who wrote the book 'The Theory of the Leisure Class' (1899) and that throwbacks to older and non-pecuniary values can also be found in both America and Japan, yet few people would locate any great economic significance in them. The declinist literature offers a fascinating and compelling exploration of social

Sorry, We Have No Money

values and cultural attributes. But it offers a weak explanation of the immediate challenges that Britain faced in the post-war period.

Rather, there were a series of distinctive features that led to a protracted decline and should be identified for what they were: policy mistakes. Moreover these were mistakes that could have been remedied by different policy actions. There were three linked errors: the adoption of Keynesian demand management with insufficient regard to the need to control inflation, which was exemplified by the decision to nationalise the Bank of England and establish a master-servant relationship between the Bank and the Treasury. This resulted in inflation, an economy losing competitiveness and the price signals in important markets such as the labour market getting distorted as well as a large sector of the economy that was nationalised. The creation of a large nationalised industry sector as part of a mixed economy, immune from competitive challenge and the normal discipline of bankruptcy, led to low productivity, over-manning, inefficiency and huge difficulty in making necessary changes and adjustment. Regional development through controls directed the geographical location of investment for many years. Administrative control prevented the location or expansion of large-scale manufacturing and business from taking place where the companies would have chosen if left to their own devices.

The role of the trade unions in the British labour market was also distinctive. Trade unions in taking strike action had a complete immunity from the conventional rules of contract and tort. The extraordinary nature of this legal position was recognised soon after the 1906 Trade Disputes Act established it. In conditions where there is a permanently accommodating monetary policy directed at securing full employment, where there was a large and expanding public sector as well as increasingly entrenched 'property rights in a job', this unusual legal position had profound implications for the role of trade unions in the labour market. Trade unions were able to bid up wages and to resist change to such an extent that inevitable change was delayed and its extent was probably greater, because of

Britain's regional problem

the lack of realism among trade union wage bargainers. The result was that the British economy did not respond swiftly or easily to changes in relative prices. Most of the change would take place in quantitative terms. Employment and output would adjust rather than wages and relative prices. And to achieve a given change in order to adjust to a real economic shock such as the development of North Sea oil, a huge change in relative prices was necessary to bring about the change in product and labour markets.

This shift in economic activity would have been difficult to manage under any circumstances, but in the context of British public policy the difficulties in the process have been aggravated rather than mitigated. Specific regional policies from the original Special Areas Acts passed in the 1930s probably hindered rather than helped and the wider context of British public policy has worked over fifty years to entrench the long process of de-industrialisation and to create the conditions for the de-marketisation of many local communities.

When industries closed, the labour market was not sufficiently flexible to enable workers to find other private sector jobs locally. In practice, the choice for most people was unemployment, or relocation or work in the public sector. An expanded public sector further eroded the role of the local market economy. From the 1950s to the 1980s trade union power set wages across all regions and in many industries, above their market clearing level. This helped to make British companies internationally uncompetitive. These were companies and industries that already found they faced difficult international competition and unrealistic national collective wage bargaining aggravated their fundamental problems. In the 1950s, 1960s and 1970s the full scale of these long-term problems was partly mitigated by direct industrial subsidies, government support for the external financing or borrowing requirements of the nationalised industries and an accommodating macroeconomic policy. That accommodating macroeconomic policy resulted in a secular decline in the sterling exchange rate that was periodically punctuated by sterling crises which pushed the exchange rate lower. The resulting inflation was high and unstable and further eroded the competitiveness of the British economy in relation to the rest of the world.

When workers were laid off they tended to have a high reservation wage. In rough terms they had a sense of what they felt they should accept in pay before they took another job. This judgement tends to be coloured by previous employment experience and an observation of the wages that other employed people are receiving locally. In Britain's regions this 'reservation wage' tended to be unrealistic, because it was based on experience drawn from working for employers covered by generous national collective agreements and from observing people working in the local public sector. Unemployment and other social security benefits which were paid at national rates took no account of regional labour markets or the regional cost of living and resulted in benefits that represented a high replacement ratio – the pay that people could realistically get by taking an available job.

When the accommodating macroeconomic environment ended in the 1980s these structural problems were fully exposed. Inflation fell sharply from around 16 per cent to 3 per cent in the early 1980s. Its re-emergence was decisively dealt with by tight domestic monetary policy from 1989 to 1990. Membership of the Exchange Rate Mechanism (ERM), further squeezed inflationary expectations and helped to entrench low inflation. This process of dramatic disinflation resulted in a huge and protracted reorganisation of the British economy. Over thirty years of delayed industrial restructuring was telescoped into some 15 years. The scale and the process were made worse by structural rigidities in the British labour market in the 1980s. Yet the puzzle is why the lost private sector and manufacturing employment was not replaced to a greater extent by other private sector market-based employment and activity.

Britain's regional problem

These regions were distinguished by:

❑ High permanent long-term unemployment;

❑ A large number of households with no employment;

❑ The migration of economically active residents often at the point of entry into the labour market; and

❑ The expansion of the public sector.

The result was that by the 1990s there were several regions that were heavily dependent on public sector employment either directly or indirectly and on social security transfer payments. While trade union reform and much more localised and realistic pay bargaining was plainly observable from the late 1980s onwards, thus removing one significant structural rigidity from the labour market, many others remained. These included the replacement ratio, non-wage social costs that employers faced as a result of regulation and local labour markets distorted by the scale and scope of the public sector.

The public sector, far from contracting, along with the contraction of the local population and economic base, if anything expanded in the regions affected by industrial decline. There are several reasons why this happened. The principal reason is that throughout the post-war period all the main public services that were provided by central government and local authorities were largely funded by central government grants. The overriding objective is to ensure broad equality of provision of health, education and social services in every part of the UK. Where local communities experienced economic decline, central government departments have introduced a succession of programmes and initiatives to address the social and economic problems involved. The result has been an increased role for the public sector in many local communities. Central government departments and agencies were also relocated to the regions, partly to save money on expensive building in the London area and partly to provide public sector jobs in the depressed regions. While trade union power and the so-called trade union mark-up has been removed as a damaging constraint

Sorry, We Have No Money

from much of the private sector in the British economy, trade union collective bargaining remains firmly entrenched in the public services and in local government.

In practice this process of de-industrialisation, combined with an entrenched and expanding powerfully unionised public sector, resulted in the further process of de-marketisation of the regional economies that is plainly evident from the early 1990s. In many of Britain's regional labour markets the combination of national social security benefits, powerful local public sector trade unions and an expanded public sector has in practice prevented a private sector adjustment where new jobs and businesses are created that partly replace the economic activity lost through de-industrialisation. Moreover, the process of de-marketisation prevents the emergence of new and internationally competitive sectors and entrenches the local role of the public sector that is funded by central government through grant and transfer payments.

This process of regional de-marketisation was given further and decisive impetus by the New Labour project of increasing public expenditure on schools, hospitals and local authority services in general. Nationally, public sector pay is higher than private sector pay. In many communities the best-paid residents are the NHS trust and local authorities' chief executives, followed by local authority chief officers, the directors of family and children's services and so on, followed by NHS consultants and local general practitioners. The public sector sets the tone for local employment and local expectations about pay and work practices. There are endemic problems with productivity, staff absence through sickness and continuing public sector employment relations and management issues.

Obtaining reliable and accurate information about regional UK GDP and the role of the private and public sectors in generating it is difficult. The best available attempt to do it has been the work done by David Smith, a former City economist who discussed regional economic performance in his inaugural lecture in 2006 as Visiting Professor of Business and Economic Forecasting at the University of Derby. What Smith shows is that when the national income figures are presented using a measure of GDP that is intended to avoid the distortions created by taxation and public expenditure, the role of the public sector is larger than it normally appears is in figures as they have been presented by the Treasury in the Budget Redbook since the 1970s. General Public Expenditure in 2004-05 represented 47.2 per cent of GDP in the UK. In its territories and several of its regions it was much higher. In Northern Ireland it was 75.8 per cent, Wales 67.9 per cent, the North East 66.4 per cent, Scotland 58.5 per cent, the North West 57.7 per cent, Yorkshire and the Humber 53 percent and the West Midlands 51.1 per cent.

The impact of the public sector can be seen through pay, industrial relations and employment. The public sector distorts regional labour markets and economies because of its size and the role that national pay bargaining and trade unions play in determining the pay and employment conditions of public sector employees. The Annual Survey of Hours and Earnings (ASHE) shows that nationally in 2009 UK median gross weekly public sector pay for full-time employees was 16 per cent higher than for private sector employees. Public sector pay was £538.9 per week, compared to private sector pay of £464.7. Given that the Labour Force Survey (LFS) suggests that a greater proportion of public sector employees work part-time it is probably more accurate to compare public and private sector earnings of all workers including those working part-time. Nationally for the UK, median gross weekly earnings for full-time and part-time employees is 12.5 per cent higher in the public sector than in the private sector – £431.1 compared to £383.3 (see Table 7.1).

Apart from the South East of England public sector pay is consistently higher than private sector pay. In the South East the difference is barely statistically significant. Public sector earnings are £421.1 per week compared to private earnings of £419.3, a difference of less than 0.5 per cent. In the East of England the public sector pay premium is 8.5 per cent, in the East Midlands 10 per cent, London 10.6 per cent, the West Midlands 12.6 per cent, Yorkshire and the Humber 12.9 per cent, the South West 14.9 per cent, the North West 17.8 per cent, Scotland 17.2 per cent, the North East 18.6 per cent and Wales 19.9 per cent.

Region	Private sector (£)	Public sector (£)	Public sector premium (%)
North East	333.7	395.8	18.6
North West	351.5	414.2	17.8
Yorkshire and the Humber	350.0	395.3	12.9
East Midlands	367.9	404.7	10.0
West Midlands	360.3	405.7	12.6
East of England	381.3	413.9	8.5
London	536.6	593.4	10.6
South East	419.3	421.1	0.4
South West	355.4	408.3	14.9
Wales	329.7	395.4	19.9
Scotland	364.0	426.7	17.2
UK	383.3	431.1	12.5

TABLE 7.1: *Median gross weekly pay for full-time and part-time employees, 2009 (£) (Source: ONS, ASHE)*

Nationally, public sector employment accounts for around a fifth of employment. The ONS article 'Regional analysis of public sector employment' (*Economic & Labour Market Review* Vol 3 No 9 September 2009) uses LFS data to look at regional variations of employment. This shows that in 2008 the UK public sector accounted for 19.8 per cent of employment. In the South East the public sector accounted for 17 per cent of employment, 17.6 per cent in the East Midlands, 17.6 in the East, 17.8 per cent in London, 19.3 per cent in the South West, 20 per cent in the West Midlands, 20.6 per cent in Yorkshire and The Humber, 20.8 per cent in the North West, 23 in the North East, 23 per cent in Scotland and 23.9 per cent in Wales and 28.8 per cent in Northern Ireland. These figures almost certainly understate the scale of public sector employment in the UK territories and regions, because public sector contracts and transfer payments are important for many local economies.

The role of traditional trade unions and collective bargaining remains entrenched in the public sector and in the least well performing regions of the UK. This partly reflects their historic manufacturing traditions, but increasingly it reflects the extent of unionisation among public sector employees. According to ONS data, around two-thirds of UK trade union members are public sector employees; 4.1 million out of a total of 6.7 million trade unions members are from the public sector. Since 1995 trade union membership has fallen from over 7 million. Private sector membership has fallen by 23 per cent. Public sector trade union membership has risen by almost 10 per cent, reflecting the expansion of public sector employment since 1997. Over half, 57.1 per cent, of public sector employees in 2009 belong to a union compared to 15.5 per cent in the private sector. Trade unions in 2009 were present in 46.6 per cent of work places. Trade union presence in the workplace was nearly three times higher among public sector employees - 85.8 per cent in 2009 - compared to the private sector where union presence was 30.2 per cent of places of employment (see Table 7.2). Likewise, 68.1 per cent of public sector employees are covered by a collective agreement compared to 17.8 per cent of private sector workers.

	Private sector (%)	Public sector (%)
Trade Union density	15.5	57.1
Trade Union presence in workplace	30.2	85.8
Employee's pay affected by a collective agreement	17.8	68.1
Trade Union wage premium	5.1	19.0

TABLE 7.2: *Trade Union influence in the workplace, 2009 (%) (Source: Trade Union Membership 2009, BIS ONS)*

The estimated trade union 'mark-up' or wage premium in the public sector was 19 per cent in 2009, compared to 5.1 per cent in the private sector. This trade union wage premium was slightly up compared to the position in 2008 when it was 2.5 per cent and 17.3 per cent in the private and public sectors. The trade union mark-up has fallen over the last twenty years, but the fall has been greatest in the private sector where it has fallen to less than a third of what it was in the mid-1990s. In the public sector there has also been a fall but it is less pronounced: a mark-up twice that of the private sector has fallen by one-third.

Public sector union density is reflected in public sector employment in the regions. In Wales in 2008 it was 67.3 per cent, Northern Ireland 66.6 per cent, Scotland 65.6 per cent and the North East of England 47.7 per cent. Private sector union density roughly followed that of the public sector. The highest private sector density was 21 per cent in Wales, with 18.7 per cent in Northern Ireland, 17.5 per cent in Scotland, 20.4 per cent in the North East of England. In contrast, the average private sector union density in England was 15 per cent, with a low of just 11.9 per cent in the South East of England.

In 2008 there were 144 stoppages of work, strikes that resulted in 758,900 working days being lost. Of these, 94 per cent were in the public sector. And 99 per cent of the days lost were disputes about pay. The role of the public sector was reflected in the distribution of the working days lost through strike action per 1,000 employees between the regions. Scotland led the way with 60, followed by the North East (54), Wales (48), the North West (38) and Yorkshire and the Humber (24). In contrast, in the East of England and the South East the figure was 7. In London, with its large number of public sector employees concentrated in the central civil service departments, the figure was 13 (see Figure 7.1).

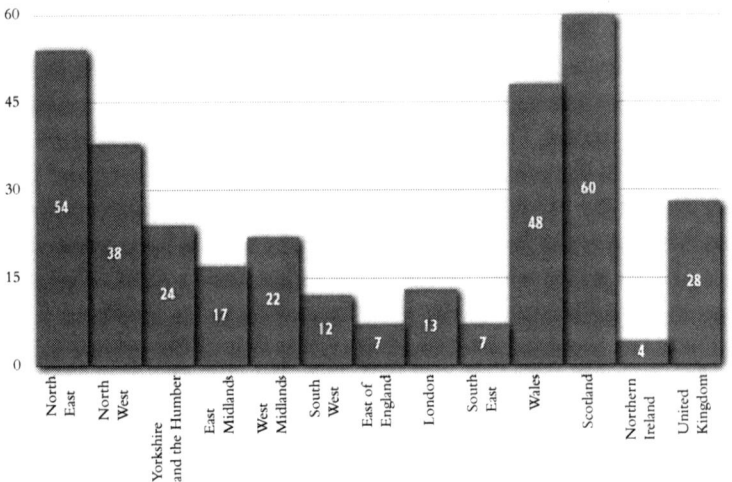

FIGURE 7.1: *Working days lost per 1,000 employees, by region, 2008 (Source: ONS Labour Market Statistics)*

In these communities private sector employers have to pay national rates of taxation, deal with national regulations and pay wages that incorporate national public sector collective pay agreements and national social security benefits. On the other hand, the potential employees locally reflect low local levels of productivity that result from local education, training, work experience and local expectations and customs. The mismatch between the tax and the employment regulation cost base of the sort associated with an advanced economy exhibiting high levels of value added compared to potential employees with few skills, and little internationally marketable training and education or work experience produces a malign dynamic of de-marketisation.

As a result of large amounts of money from central government, the scale of regional and regeneration policy is evident to any observant visitor to Britain's great northern cities, such as Liverpool and Manchester. Their magnificent Victorian and in the case of Liverpool often Georgian city centre buildings look as architecturally impressive as ever. Yet it is not at all clear that the restoration of buildings such as St George's Hall in Liverpool has been matched by a commensurate improvement in local social and economic indicators. To paraphrase Bertholt Brecht, it appears that the buildings have been regenerated, but the people have not.

In fact a reference to Brecht and East Germany is apposite in any contemporary discussion of the performance of the UK's regional economies. In a completely different political, economic and social context the UK and the German Democratic Republic have in practice dealt with depressed regions undergoing awkward and concentrated economic transitions in similar ways and with similarly disappointing outcomes. At first glance such a suggestion might appear to be a piece of polemical rhetoric, but on careful analysis the parallels are telling.

In 1937 the East German *Länder* that were formerly part of the GDP performed as well economically as the rest of Germany, if anything they were slightly more prosperous than the western regions of the old Reich. By 1989 however, when properly measured, the residents of the GDR enjoyed a per capita GDP that was about one-third of their western neighbours. Unification in 1990 was accompanied by a series of economic decisions that made an internationally uncompetitive economy, with very low rates of productivity and market value added, even less competitive:

- One-for-one monetary union gave GDR consumers the economic power to buy high-quality goods manufactured anywhere in the world and preferably not in either the GDR or any other Soviet satellite economy.

- It made East German goods even more uncompetitive internationally and in particular it made its exports to its former trading partners in the east uncompetitive. Overall, East German goods became uncompetitive at home and even more uncompetitive abroad. So the economy of the former GDR lost both its export market and a large share of its domestic market.

- To prevent East German workers competing against West German workers and threatening West German wages or employment conditions, the unions insisted that West German national collective pay bargaining and employment regulation should be extended to the east. The result was that West German pay rates were progressively extended to East Germany.

- West German social security was extended to East Germany to protect workers who found themselves displaced during the transition process.

The combination of a strong and rising exchange rate, a huge increase in wages towards West German levels plus higher social security transfer payments on the West German model was a recipe for high unemployment and a high replacement ratio that resulted in permanent and entrenched structural unemployment.

- In 1990, at the start of the transition process, of all the former communist countries the citizens of the GDR appeared to be the best placed.

- The GDR was widely perceived as the most modern and efficient of the former socialist planned economies.

- By uniting with its western neighbour it immediately received all the institutional benefits of the rule of law, democratic institutions, an independent judiciary and a proper framework for competition policy.

Sorry, We Have No Money

❏ The East German economy would receive massive support from the West German taxpayer. There would be money for investment, modernisation and to support people displaced by the transition process.

It was as though the Marshall Plan was being resurrected just for East Germany. Some of the GDR's former trading partners, with some envy, more pejoratively expressed it as having the benefits of a generous sugar-daddy next door.

The transfer payments involved were indeed huge. They represented about 3 or 4 per cent of West German GDP each year. In relation to East Germany they were much more significant – after taking account of production subsidies, transfers appear to have accounted for over half of GDP per capita. Half of these transfer payments were in the form of social security benefits. About a quarter of East German consumption was financed by West German transfers. In the East the transition process was swift. The Treuhand agency set up in 1990 employed a combination of sale, break-up and closure. This process of privatisation was much faster than in other transition economies. Part of the explanation for the speed was that generous social security transfer payments protected East German residents that lost their jobs. Between 1989 and 1992 employment roughly halved. Far from East German living standards falling they rose rapidly, because West German social security benefits were worth a great deal more than East German wages were before 1989. While unemployment rose and remained high, incomes rose. By the mid-1990s East German household income was about 80 per cent of West German income, but progress in raising incomes closer to the German average since then has been very slow and disappointing.

The process of privatisation in some respects mirrored the process of de-industrialisation in Britain's regions. Manufacturing industries were closed down, scaled back and sold off to outside investors. Inward investment was attracted to the former GDR from West Germany. In the same way, inward investment was attracted into the UK from countries such as Japan. In both cases this investment brought with it much-needed capital, facilitated technology transfer and the introduction of new skills and working practices. There was also both in East Germany and in the British regions a perception that investors from outside that bought business took what they wanted and often simply closed the rest down. The overwhelming effect of this economic re-organisation was the radical reduction in economic activity largely through closure. In East Germany twenty years later unemployment is over 14 per cent, more than twice the rate in the west.

Twenty years after the transition started there is increasing recognition in Germany that the combination of inflexible wages, high social costs and generous social security benefits (that result in a high replacement ratio) have created a dependent non-market economy. This analysis is perhaps best summarised in a paper from the Kiel Institute written by Christian Merkl and Denis Snower that benefits from the arresting title of 'The Caring Hand That Cripples: The East German Labour Market After Unification' (1996). They argue that the high levels of structural unemployment and the failure of the private sector to thrive has not been an accident but rather the direct result of the public sector support that the East German regions have received. Other transition economies are now starting to catch up with East Germany and to overhaul it. Many of them have a better track record in terms of unemployment and employment. Slovenia became the first transition economy to have a higher GDP per capita than East Germany. There is anecdotal evidence that some Polish communities that border East Germany have higher employment, higher earnings and higher house prices and rents.

Merkl and Snower believe that the East German case is important because it highlights the weaknesses of other European welfare systems. It exemplifies how communities and whole regions can fall into a form of public sector-financed dependency where the principal drivers that determine incomes and prosperity are largely

Sorry, We Have No Money

detached from the market economy. Merkl and Snower argue that this arises because labour force participations fall into a series of related but principally benefit-driven traps. These concern low skills, an ageing workforce, the replacement of workers by labour-saving capital, along with skills and capital under-utilisation and unemployment rising from the decline of the tradable or market sector. The OECD's 2009 'Fact Book' of social and economic indicators shows that within the UK there is a very wide dispersion of income between its regions. The latest available figures for per capita GDP expressed in purchasing power parities indicates that Wales, Northern Ireland and the North East of England have incomes of only 80 per cent of those of the UK average, while the North West, Yorkshire and the Humber and the West Midlands have incomes around 87 per cent of the UK average. Taxation and social security transfer payments significantly raise household incomes in these weak performing regions and territories. The figures for regional household income show that Welsh households had incomes equivalent to 88 per cent of the UK average, despite having a GDP per capita generated in Wales of less than 80 per cent. There is a similar story for Northern Ireland, the North East and the North West and Yorkshire and the Humber. This picture of entrenched regional dispersion of economic activity with household incomes grossed up by transfer payments appears to be uncomfortably close to the East German experience since 1990.

Moreover, since 1998 and the increases in public expenditure, the establishment of the regional development agencies and a succession of regeneration programmes, the dispersion of in-regional economic activity has become greater and more entrenched compared to the mid-1990s. The ONS regional gross value added (GVA) statistics show that the role of the London economy has increased. The role of Scottish, East Midlands, North East, North West and Yorkshire and the Humber economies have contracted in terms of total share of total GVA that is generated, comparing 2008 with 1995 (see Figure 7.2). In terms of GVA per head of population

Britain's regional problem

compared to the UK average, between 1995 and 2008 it fell in every territory and region apart from the South West and Northern Ireland where it was broadly unchanged, and London and the South East where it rose (see Figure 7.3).

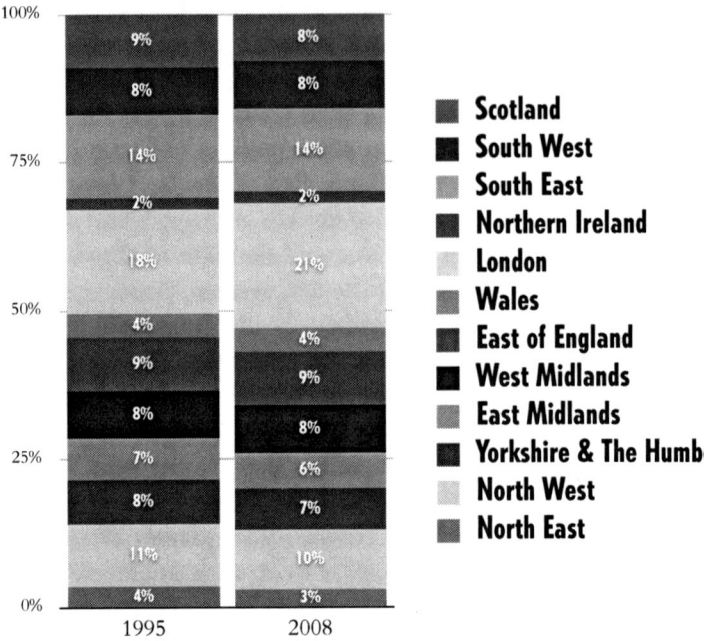

FIGURE 7.2: *Regional shares of total GVA, 1995 and 2008 (Source: ONS)*

Sorry, We Have No Money

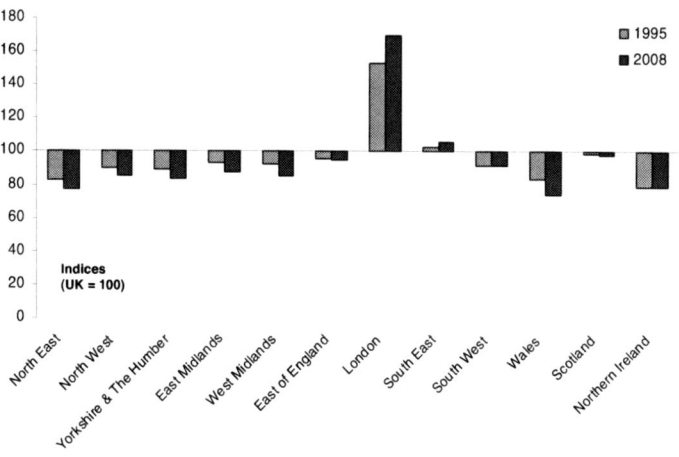

FIGURE 7.3: *Regional GVA per head indices compared to UK average, 1995 and 2008 (Source: ONS)*

Professor Alison Wolf provides an excellent analysis of the consequences of large public sectors dominating regional economies in parts of the UK and in East Germany. In her monograph 'More than we bargained for: the social and economic costs of national wage bargaining' (2010) she locates the principal cause in nationally determined public sector pay and explores its consequences. Public sector services are provided throughout the UK to ensure a broad similarity of provision. Yet the regions themselves are very different in terms of their level of economic activity and the productivity of the local labour markets. National pay scales in the public sector do not relate to local labour market conditions in the UK regions. Large public sectors in the regions and high-paying public sector jobs in deprived cities and regions have been perceived by the public sector as part of the solution to the problem of poorly performing economic regions, whereas Alison Wolf argues that they aggravate these regional economic problems because they undermine one of the few advantages that relatively deprived and unsuccessful localities have. Such policies make it harder for them to catch up.

Wolf has separately written extensively on the economics of education and training. She argues that the last Labour government's policy prescription to remedy the weak performance of Britain's poor performing regions was through a 'supply-side' remedy. This version of supply-side economics was increased spending on education and training to raise the number of people with formal educational qualifications and to increase benefits testing to oblige people to search for work more actively, which would then reduce regional inequalities in employment and income. Wolf points out that such policies fail to take account of the fact that employment prospects for people in different regions vary for any given level of education and qualification. The issue is not simply that people in economically unsuccessful regions have lower average levels of attainment among school students and in their general population, which they do, but more importantly that people find it more difficult to get work for any given level of education than they would in a more dynamic region.

The policy of trying to tackle structural under-employment through vocational training has been at the heart of regional economic policy for over twenty years and appears to have had little if any impact. Ken Mayhew et al in 'From Skills Revolution to Productivity Miracle – Not as easy as it Sounds?' (_Oxford Review of Economic Policy, 2006_) showed that there were no financial returns to adults who acquire additional vocational qualifications. Esra Erdem and Andrew Glyn in 'Job deficits in the UK regions' (2001) point out that the severity of regional employment problems contradicts the picture of the UK labour market being highly flexible. They found that the gap in employment rates for the least qualified between the South East of England and the North, notably Merseyside and Tyneside, are as great as in East Germany. They found that in the 1990s despite a general expansion of the economy in terms of non-employment as opposed to unemployment the regional

**Sorry, We Have No Money**

dispersion actually increased and was greatest among younger people aged 15-24 and 25-34 in the bottom quarter of the earnings distribution. The implication of Erdem and Glyn's research is that public policy over the last thirty years has entrenched and compounded these regional disparities because younger people are affected worse than their parents and grandparents, whose generation experienced de-industrialisation directly.

The late Andrew Glyn was a Marxist economist who provocatively analysed the profits squeeze in the 1970s and also realised how a serious crisis of capitalist accumulation was turned around by the Thatcher administration in the 1980s. In short, Andrew Glyn could identify a structural problem when he came across one. It was Glyn's work that alerted Alison Wolf to the analogy between the UK's regions and the former GDR regions. Some journalists have described these UK regions as having almost Soviet-style economies. While that is a vivid way of drawing attention to the large public sectors in these regions and raising the important issue of the extent to which they are de-marketised, it is a misleading and distorting exaggeration. Those regions may depend on public sector transfer payments, but have full access to international markets and make decisions about the use of resources that are properly priced in conventional market terms. For example, they face normal internationally decided market prices for energy consumption. This means that the scale of distortions and the sort of systematic welfare losses generated for many years in the socialist planned economies are not present. The problems instead are principally located in a heavily distorted labour market.

The heart of the UK's regional economic problem is that individuals and communities have progressively become de-marketised over the last thirty years. If anything, public policy measures intended to mitigate social and economic deprivation have aggravated the problem. The combination of large and expanding public sector employers paying nationally agreed salaries, a national social security benefits system that destroys work incentives even in generally high performing labour markets such as London, and expensive national regulatory and tax burdens makes the regions uncompetitive internally and externally. The UK public sector has ignored the role of relative prices and pursued polices that assume that simply spending public money can overcome the handicap of local labour markets where wages are not able to adjust to the productivity in the local economy. It has been plain for many years that the British economy needs greater regional pay differentials and the critical thing is to change public sector pay settlement arrangements so that public sector pay reflects conditions in regional labour markets.

Sorry, We Have No Money

Chapter 8: Centralised public sector pay bargaining and public sector pensions

HISTORICALLY THE UK HAS BEEN UNUSUALLY CENTRALISED, even for a unitary nation state. The UK is no longer a unitary state; there are significant measures of devolution in the Scotland, Wales and Northern Ireland, 'the territories' as the Treasury used to call them. England, however, remains highly centralised. What is more its large public sector has a highly centralised system of pay bargaining. Devolution has complicated the picture; however, throughout the UK public sector pay bargaining is generally centralised. In a few areas public sector pay is determined nationally solely for England and in others it is decided centrally for one or more parts of the UK.

OECD economies are distinguished by several shared characteristics:

- High levels of GDP per capita;
- Large and expensive public sectors;
- Significant although falling trade union membership; and
- Consistently higher levels of trade union membership in the public sector.

Historically many OECD countries had centralised pay bargaining both for private sector and public sector employees. Over the last thirty years centralised pay setting arrangements for the private sector have significantly declined throughout the OECD. Centralised pay bargaining has increasingly been the preserve of the public sector. In the UK, trade union membership has fallen and the proportion of workers covered by collective agreements has fallen. Most trade union members are public sector employees and are women, reflecting the feminisation of the labour market as public sector employment has expanded.

An ONS article 'The changing face of public sector employment 1999–2009' (*Economic & Labour Market Review* Vol 4 No7 July 2010) shows that in the ten years to 2009 both public sector pay and employment rose. The share of public sector employment within total employment rose and the public sector head count rose along with the pay premium that public sector employees enjoy (see Figures

8.1. and 8.2). As a result of the banking crisis and the nationalisation of the banks some 230,000 jobs were reclassified as being in the public sector. By removing the banks from estimates of public sector employment, it is still clear that public sector employment has grown significantly, showing an upward trend of 12 per cent between 1999 and 2009.

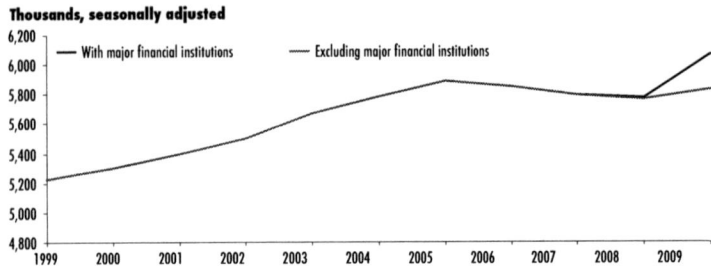

FIGURE 8.1: *UK public sector employment head count including and excluding the major financial institutions, 1999–2009 (Source: ONS, ELMR, Vol 4 No 7 July 2010)*

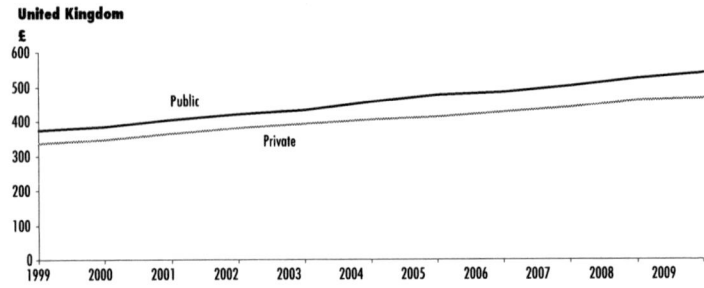

FIGURE 8.2: *Median gross weekly earnings for full-time employees, 1999–2009 (Source: ONS, ELMR, Vol 4 No 7 July 2010)*

Alison Wolf (in 'More than we bargained for: the social and economic costs of national wage bargaining') has constructed a detailed taxonomy of the numbers and categories of public sector workers covered by central pay setting arrangements. The data from the 2004 'Workplace Employment Relations Survey' indicated that 92 per cent of public sector managers had to follow policy on pay agreed elsewhere in their organisation. She concludes that it is reasonable to assume that at least 80 per cent of public sector workers are covered by national agreements, which means that in England at least a fifth of jobs are covered by centralised public sector terms and conditions.

National collective pay agreements set the terms and conditions of between 4.6–5 million people in England. Local authority employees are covered by the National Joint Council for Local Government Services. Through the Single Status Agreement made in 1997 that body set the pay for 1.4 million council workers. National pay review bodies set the pay and working conditions of teachers, dentists, doctors, nurses, other health professionals, and the police. The Office of Manpower Economics, the secretariat that supports the pay review bodies, estimates that these agreements cover 1.8 million people. Universities are not obliged by law to participate in national pay setting arrangements, but choose to do so. 198,000 employees are covered by the Joint Negotiating Committee for Higher Education Staff. Further education colleges are not obliged to participate in national pay arrangements but most do so through the National Joint Forum, which covers the pay of some 200,000 employees in FE colleges and sixth form colleges. Civil servants' pay is determined by departments on the basis of a nationally agreed pay spine established in the 1990s. These arrangements apply to 500,000 civil servants, about three quarters of whom work outside of London and the South East of England. National agreements cover 176,000 Royal Mail employees and some 380,000 school support staff.

Pay review bodies cover 40 per cent of public sector workers. Alison Wolf points out that these bodies do not just look at pay, but a wider set of issues such as job flexibility and gender equality. There has been a tendency to try and simplify and at the same time re-evaluate the pay of jobs in the sectors covered by the pay review bodies. For all workers in the NHS (apart from doctors, dentists and some categories of manager) progression is linked to the nationally agreed Knowledge and Skills Framework. The universities have a similar modernisation agenda that involves placing all but the most senior employees on a national 51-point scale, then evaluating every job for its content and contribution, and then changing pay as appropriate.

This approach to setting pay is a recipe for increasing the bill. Pay is not determined by individual performance but by the previous starting point and there is a tendency to upgrade jobs in the evaluation rather than to demote them. As Alison Wolf points out, it is always more popular when departments raise pay than when they cut it. There is a powerful incentive to find ways of avoiding cutting people's pay while feeling obliged to raise the pay of people who appear to be unfavourably treated compared to others. This asymmetry is compounded in a period of rapidly rising public expenditure where the budget constraint is significantly weakened. The National Audit Office concluded that the new pay arrangements in the NHS probably did not have a major direct impact on the wage bill because expenditure was rising sharply. The University and Colleges Employers' Association indicates the modernisation agenda had raised pay for 8.6 per cent of academics and 15 per cent of support staff, while 2.4 per cent of academics and 6.8 per cent of support staff had their pay frozen because their pay was too high. Across the public sector the pay modernisation agenda has generated significant pay increases and big pay increases for low-paid employees.

Alison Wolf's conclusion is that there has been a big increase in the scope and the coverage of national agreements, involving the conditions as well as the pay of public sector workers. As a result, the English labour market exhibits to an unusual extent national pay setting arrangements that cover a large proportion of the workforce. These arrangements, combined with the modernisation agenda and a reluctance of public sector mangers to antagonise

Sorry, We Have No Money

the workforce, in the context of potentially forceful trade union opposition, have both raised public sector pay and public spending and ensured that increases in expenditure were, as the OECD had warned, absorbed in public sector price inflation rather than used to raise public sector output.

Public sector pensions

PUBLIC SECTOR WORKERS enjoy generous pension arrangements. There are two types of occupational pension. Defined benefit schemes offer to pay a pension linked to salary and length of service. The higher the final salary and the longer the period of employment the higher the pension. Defined contribution schemes pay out a sum based on the value of a person's fund on retirement. The pension will be determined by the amount paid in and the investment return. Most public sector employees are in defined benefit schemes and usually pension benefits are based on either 1/160th or 1/180th of the final salary for each year of service.

The five largest public service schemes operate on a pay as you go basis. These are the armed forces, civil service, NHS, police and teachers pension funds. The Government Actuary's Department estimated that in 2007-08 they had a combined membership of around 7 million people. These include 3.2 million contributing employed members, 2.3 million pensioners - including survivors - and 1.6 million early leavers with deferred pensions. By any conventional measure these pension schemes are large – the NHS, which has 2.74 million members, is the world's largest single occupational pension fund, reflecting the NHS's position as the world's third largest employer.

The main funded public pension scheme that holds cash, bond and long-term investment assets such as equities is the Local Government Pension Scheme. This had 3.9 million members in 2008-09, made up of 1.7 million employed members, 1.1 million deferred members and 1.1 million pensioner members. The funding for local authority pensions is unusual in being funded and reflects the recommendation of a committee that discussed local authority pension schemes in 1919.

The Pay As You Go schemes have no investment assets. Instead the employer and employee pay contributions to the sponsoring government department, which pays benefits to the pensioners netting off the contributions received. The Armed Forces scheme is unusual in that employees make no contribution, although their pay review body takes account of this when setting their pay. In some public sector schemes contributions from active employed members and employers exceed the cost of the pensions being paid out. The NHS in 2007-08 had contributions of £6.9 billion, comfortably exceeding the pension bill of £4.9 billion. This reflects the expansion of the NHS employment in recent years. In 2010-11 net payments will overall exceed contributions by £4.6 billion. This is a fourfold increase from 2006-07 when the net payment was £1.1 billion.

The gross liability or stock of pay as you go public sector pension funds was estimated by the Treasury in March 2008 to be £770 billion. That figure is the total value of benefits accrued up until the end of March 2008 and due to be paid over a period of 60 to 70 years to around 7 million public sector employees, former employees and their dependents. This estimate used the same accounting framework that actuaries use for private sector schemes: FRS 17/ IAS 19. It converts future cash flow payments into a single figure and applies a discount rate. The resulting cash lump sum is how much needs to be invested today to pay out benefits in the future. An increase in the discount rate has the effect of reducing pension liabilities and a reduction in the discount rate increases them. The total liability figure is therefore highly sensitive to changes in the discount rate. The public sector pension liability has increased from £425 billion in 2003 to £770 billion in 2008. This increase reflected things like increased life expectancy. The last Labour government described them as largely resulting from 'technical' and

Sorry, We Have No Money

'accounting' effects rather than increases in the pensions being paid. But these technical and accounting effects reflected real costs of paying the pensions themselves and it is the cash bill that has to be funded that is important.

The last Labour government preferred to emphasise the annual cost of public sector pensions in the future as a share of annual GDP. The Treasury projected that the share of GDP taken by public sector pensions would rise from 1.5 per cent of GDP in 2008 to 2 per cent by 2027-28, remaining just under 2 per cent thereafter. The projected rise reflected recent increases in public sector employment, increased life expectancy and the fact that the spending on NHS pensions had yet to come through given its increased employment. As Lord Turner, chairman of the Pensions Committee (2003–06), commented, increasing the share of national income taken by public sector by a third is 'significant'.

As well as the debate about the scale and cost of public sector pensions there is increasing interest in whether the Treasury has accurately calculated the total cost of its liabilities and whether the future costs of its public pension commitments have been underestimated. The discount rate used is the same as that used for FRS 17 and accords to market funding conditions. It is based on an AA rated corporate bond rate. Neil Record, a former Bank of England economist, has pointed out that a more appropriate discount rate would be the index-linked gilt rate, on the basis that this reflects the true cost of government borrowing. Given that it is lower than the AA corporate bond rate, it would have the effect of increasing the liabilities of public sector pension schemes. The Treasury has lamely argued against this on the grounds that it would set it apart from other schemes. That of course neglects the fact that the public sector is currently set apart both by the generosity of its arrangements and the 'gilt-edged' credit that secures these index-linked schemes.

The 81 funded local authority schemes at the end of March 2007 had assets of £132 billion and liabilities of £159 billion; they were

Centralised public sector pay bargaining and public sector pensions

about 83 per cent funded with an unfunded cash liability of £27 billion.

The state national insurance basic pension and its other related benefits such as incapacity benefit and maternity benefit paid from the National Insurance Fund amounted to £70.5 billion in 2008. These benefits are financed on a pay as you go basis and are unfunded. In 2003 the Treasury estimated that the state pension scheme presented a liability of £1,170 billion.

Public sector pay has risen significantly over the last decade and with it future pension fund liabilities have increased. At the same time the extent, coverage and generosity of private sector occupational schemes has been reduced. The number of defined benefit schemes has fallen and there has been a significant move towards defined contribution schemes where the principal risks are taken by the employee rather than by the employer. Attempts to systematically reform public sector pensions have encountered entrenched trade union opposition. In 2005 the Labour government agreed a number of changes with the unions to rein in the cost of public sector pensions. These include measures to cap and share the cost of public sector schemes and raising the pension age to 65 from 60 for new entrants. These changes are estimated by the Treasury to save £1 billion a year from 2013-12 and will double over the long term. Yet such savings are very modest in terms of future pension liabilities.

Public sector pay in the UK in 2008 was £174 billion, representing 30 per cent of total government spending and 12 per cent of GDP. Over the last forty years public sector pay has fallen from a peak of 22 per cent of GDP to a low of 11 per cent in 1999. This fall reflected the privatisation of public sector corporations, the reduction in public expenditure as a share of national income and the reduction in the level of public sector employment. The IFS, in the 2010 Green Budget, shows how changes in the public sector wage bill are influenced by the number of people employed – the head count and the average wage cost per employee:

Sorry, We Have No Money

- Between 1979 and 1997 each year the head count fell by on average by 2 per cent, while the real cost per head rose by 1.6 per cent a year;

- Between 1997 and 2008 the head count rose by 1 per cent a year and the cost per head rose by 2.6 per cent;

- Most of the increase in the public sector pay bill took place between 2000 and 2005, when the head count rose by 3 per cent a year.

The Labour Force Survey suggests that public sector employment rose by 12 per cent between 1997 and 2008:

- The biggest rise was in NHS employment, which rose 27 per cent with 29 per cent more nurses and 49 per cent more doctors;

- The number of police rose by 24 per cent;

- Education employment rose by 23 per cent, with the number of teachers rising by 9 per cent, while the number of teaching assistants rose by 260 per cent;

- The number of public sector administrators rose by 7 per cent and there were some examples of contraction;

- The armed services fell by 12 per cent.

Since 1997 public sector pay has risen sharply relative to private sector pay. The IFS shows that in 2005-06, before the labour market was cyclically distorted by the frozen money markets in 2007 and the slump in output that started in 2008, the public sector offered a premium compared to the private sector of between 15 per cent for men and 22 per cent for women. In the Green Budget the IFS regards these figures as 'raw' and does not believe that they compare like with like, and that when a comparison is made between the public and private sectors that takes account of the composition of the workforces the public sector premium narrows significantly. The IFS suggests that once that is done the public sector premium falls to 2 per cent for men and 4 per cent for women. The IFS, drawing on other work done by Richard Disney and Amanda

Gosling, adjusts the comparison to take account of the composition of the public and private sector workforces in terms of educational qualifications, gender and age and concludes that changes in the composition of the public sector workforce do not appear to have driven the increase in the pay differential, but rather the pay differential has come to reflect the changes in the public sector.

The IFS estimates that in regions distant from London, public sector wages are high compared to the private sector. Controlling for and taking account of education, age and qualifications outside of London and the South East of England the average public sector worker enjoys a 5 per cent wage premium for men and 11 per cent for women.

The difficulty with the IFS analysis of public sector pay is that the public sector did not simply start to employ more teachers, nurses, doctors and managers who were more qualified and educated by an evolutionary, organic, almost accidental process. This happened because of a combination of increased discretionary spending, generous pay settlements and a pay modernisation agenda that worked to increase public sector pay. There was then a sustained relative price effect that is particularly pronounced in the devolved territories and the English regions that resulted in more graduates and better qualified people working in the public sector because the pay was better.

Yet even on the IFS analysis of an adjusted public sector pay premium of 5 per cent – 2 per cent for men and 7 per cent for women – the cash consequence is around £5.5 billion on the IFS's own estimate. While the IFS argues that the wage premiums are on a like-for-like basis exaggerated by the raw data, it is unequivocal about the generosity of the pensions enjoyed by public sector employees. Public sector employees are much more likely to be members of an occupational pension scheme and a defined benefits pension scheme than the private sector employees. On average public sector defined benefits schemes are more generous than those in the private sector and the relative generosity of public pension provision has increased relative to that of the private sector as private schemes have closed down and their benefits have been cut.

The IFS estimates that 85 per cent of public sector employees are covered by occupational pension schemes of whom 95 per cent are in defined contribution schemes. This means that 78 per cent of all public sector employees enjoy the benefits of a defined benefit scheme. In the private sector around 40 per cent of employees are covered by an employer-sponsored occupational pension and only 15 per cent of private sector employees have a defined benefit pension. Over the last thirty years the number of private sector employees who are members of defined contribution schemes has roughly halved, from almost 6 million employees to around 2.25 million. And the numbers of private sector employees with such defined benefit schemes are continuing to fall. Only 38 per cent of private sector defined benefit schemes are open to new members.

The value of a defined benefit pension is on average worth more to public sector workers than private sector workers. IFS research shows that a public sector scheme is worth on average 26 per cent of earnings, whereas a private defined benefit scheme is worth 19 per cent of earnings on average. This relative generosity arises from the fact that the pensionable age is lower for the majority who entered the public sector before 2007 and because of differences in earning profile over a working life. In the private sector earnings rise sharply at the start and then tail off, whereas in the public sector earnings continue to grow, so that with a defined benefit scheme based on the final salary the resulting occupational pension is worth more.

When comparing contributions and benefits, public sector pensions are worth significantly more than private sector occupational arrangements. The IFS estimates that the difference is worth 12 per cent of earnings and that taken with the adjusted wage premium, public sector workers enjoy at least a 12 per cent premium in their total pay and pension remuneration. Given that the IFS estimates that the public sector enjoys an estimated 2 per cent wage premium, this suggests on the basis of the IFS adjusted pay analysis that the premium is at least 14 per cent.

In 2007 and 2008 the government agreed new rules that raised the retirement age for public sector workers: nurses, teachers, civil servants and local authority employees would now have a usual retirement age of 65 rather than 60. The infamous Rule of 85 in local authority pensions effectively made retirement at 60 on a full pension the norm and in many cases workers went before. But these changes only take effect on new members, not on exiting public sector employees in the largest funded schemes and will have no impact until the 2040s. The civil service pension scheme will move for new entrants from a final salary scheme to a career average scheme. Overall, these changes will reduce the value of the pension for the main public sector schemes from 23 to 20 per cent of earnings for new entrants into the public sector. The police, fire service and armed services have separate arrangements that will continue to be worth 33 per cent of average earnings for new entrants and 39 per cent for existing members. In addition in 2009 the Treasury announced the new cap-and-share arrangements whereby increases in benefits arising out of higher than expected pay or increased life expectancy will be shared by higher employer and employee contribution rates.

The IFS's conclusion is that these are only 'very modest reforms' which will, for new entrants only, close about half the gap between the average generosity of the public and private sector schemes. They will not of course, make any difference to the gap in coverage between public and private.

The heart of the UK public sector pay premium compared to the private sector is not some elaborate matter turning on the composition of the state workforce compared to that of the economy as a whole, but a continuing trade union influence that is able to extract a wage premium. Both Conservative and Labour governments in the 1990s and 2000s have been reluctant to confront or irritate public sector employees. Alison Wolf points out that the single status framework based on a national pay spine for local government was negotiated under a Conservative government in the run-up to the 1997 general election. Wolf quotes S Bach, K Givan and J Forth's judgment in 'The Public Sector in Transition' (2009) that there was a retreat from local pay bargaining within the NHS from the 1990s because of 'managerial reluctance to antagonise the workforce in a context of forceful union opposition, alongside limited managerial skills and severe financial constraints'.

Labour extended national pay arrangements to school support staff, including that for support staff in academies that are not obliged to use national pay arrangements for their other staff. Wolf's judgment is that the pay modernisation agenda has resulted in 'big increases for lower paid and especially female employees'. Moreover, Wolf points out that in the context of a national pay scheme, successful wage claims made in one locality as part of the equality agenda have 'enormous, unpredictable and country-wide repercussions'. Public sector pay for manual employees and the low skilled is significantly higher than in the private sector. This is all a long way from the public sector catching up with the private sector, matching private sector pay in the long term and reflecting the composition of the skills base of the public and private sectors. It has been much more about producer interests and public sector trade unions engaging in effective and sustained rent seeking. It is difficult not to conclude that there are now many employees in the public sector who are currently enjoying an 'economic rent' in excess of they pay that they could realistically expect to receive in the private sector. John Philpot, the economic adviser to the Chartered Institute of Personnel and Development, has said (*Financial Times*, 30 June 2010) that private sector employers would be reluctant to hire employees displaced from the public sector, not just because of uncertainty about the economic outlook, but because of a perception that long-term public sector workers lacked initiative.

Centralised public sector pay bargaining and public sector pensions

Chapter 9: Social security transfer payments and age-related spending

THE UK SPENDS AROUND 13 PER CENT OF GDP on social security benefits.

In a market economy there is bound to be a wide dispersion of earnings and output and incomes are unstable because of the economic cycle. Many households will not be in a position to finance a level of consumption that is generally acceptable to society at large. The public sector through social security transfer payments quite rightly mitigates this. The public sector can help smooth incomes over the life cycle and offer people who encounter difficulty as a result of unemployment or sickness help when they need it. In periods when output falls, unemployment benefits should play a useful role as automatic stabilisers helping to maintain demand.

At its best, a properly operating social security system enables market economies to work by protecting people in difficult circumstances and providing people with a safety net that enables them to take risk and supports spending in recessions. Social security benefits also have malign consequences. Such transfer payments modify the incentives that households have to work and save and have important consequences for the supply of labour. These effects arise directly out of the benefits themselves and the tax burden needed to finance them. Social insurance systems create changes in behaviour, in the same way that private insurance markets exhibit moral hazard.

The changing nature of the causes of poverty

TRADITIONALLY THE MAIN SOURCES OF POVERTY were associated with the temporary loss of income as a result of the loss of earnings through sickness or unemployment and the absence of earnings in old age when people ceased to work. Over the last thirty years families on low incomes with children became the principal source of poverty. From its start the welfare state was intended to help people with old age, experiencing temporary unemployment or sickness. It was never intended to replace the need for individuals to

Social security transfer payments and age-related spending

take responsibility for making their own provision. Although from the start for many below-average income households the range of state benefits became the basic level that households expected to rely on and they did not make the degree of systematic additional provision that Lord Beveridge expected. This was partly because the basic minimum unemployment insurance and old age pension became supplemented by additional means-tested benefits for low income households or households that did not have a pattern of national insurance contributions that entitled them to the conventional insurance benefits. Moreover, the means-tested benefits became more generous than the basic entitlement. This created a moral hazard where people who saved or worked and built up national insurance contributions were little or no better off at low levels of income than households that had not done so.

Structural unemployment, unemployment and poverty traps

IN THE 1970S and 1980s in the UK and European economies it became increasingly apparent that social security benefits significantly modified labour market institutions and created the conditions where people could be permanently unemployed regardless of the state of the economic cycle and the level of demand in the economy. This structural unemployment became an entrenched feature of many EU economies. The level of social security benefits for an increasing number of households undermined the incentive to work because the realistic after-tax income is low compared with the level of benefits that would be given up. The measure that offers some guidance here is the replacement ratio. This measures the level of out-of-work benefits compared to in-work earnings. In the UK, social security replacement ratios have fallen little since the 1970s when the average replacement rate was 60 per cent. In the 1980s and 1990s Conservative governments took a series of measures to lower the ratio and to improve the incentive to partici-pate in the labour market. Given that the actual ratio interacts with things such as rents and earnings, the IFS has estimated that the average replacement ratio only fell to 56 per cent by the mid-1990s and has remained broadly stable at that level since then. Between 1997 and 2010, labour market and other policy measures generally worked to raise it and damage incentives. These average replace-ment ratios of around 56 per cent have a powerful influence on the labour supply in individual communities and regions where realis-tic private sector earnings are significantly lower than the national average.

In helping households in poverty or in smoothing their in-comes over the life cycle, governments confront a choice. They either provide universal benefits that are paid to everyone regard-less of income, or they provide carefully targeted benefits that are means-tested or targeted by category of circumstance. There are advantages and practical problems with both. Means-tested benefits are targeted and a relatively inexpensive way of helping people in terms of total public expenditure, which means that they can offer more generous help, but as income rises they are withdrawn, which has an adverse effect on incentives. For people of working age that creates poverty and unemployment traps. In some circumstances, the withdrawal of a benefit could make a person pound for pound worse off so that it would pay them not to work, the so-called 'un-employment trap'. In others, a more generous rate of withdrawal interacts with taxes to create a poverty trap, where even significant increases in pay are of little value to people once deductions are made. The choice for policy makers is broadly between having a small portion over the earnings range where there are very high net rates of withdrawal that affect a smaller number of households, or a much gentler rate of withdrawal that draws many more house-holds into what are still high rates of withdrawal of income. The latter in public expenditure terms tends to be more expensive, be-cause more households continue to receive benefits further up the earnings distribution. The principal targeted benefits are the Working Families Tax credit, Housing Benefit and the Pensioner Credit.

In contrast, universal benefits have fewer of the direct malign effects that means-tested or targeted benefits have, but they are very expensive. The more generous they become, the more they will have a damaging and distorting effect on the economy through the taxes that are necessary to pay for them. Expensive universal provision of social security transfer payments such as the old age basic pension, child benefit, and 'in kind' services such as health and education, result in an overall tax burden that travels a long way down the earnings distribution. People are then drawn into paying income tax at low multiples of average earnings. Many find themselves paying tax while at the same time being in receipt of means-tested benefits.

The interaction between tax thresholds and marginal tax rates and the rules governing the net rates of withdrawal of housing benefit and the payments from tax credits are so complicated that significant and worthwhile polices such as raising the income tax threshold to £10,000 have much less effect on many households, because what they gain in lower taxes is offset by other higher rates of withdrawal. It is very difficult to make changes to the system on a cost neutral basis without creating losers. Improving incentives and eliminating distortions without creating losers is expensive.

The damaging effect of means-tested benefits and tax credits

THE SYSTEM OF TAX CREDITS was introduced in 1998 and has undergone many complex changes. It has increased the help given to households in work and to households with children in particular. But this assistance has come at a heavy cost in terms of public spending and labour market incentives. Spending on tax credits is now £24 billion. The number of households where there is a net rate of benefit withdrawal greater than 60 per cent has more than doubled from 750,000 in 1996-97 to 1,895,000 in 2010-11. After changes made in the Emergency Budget in June 2010 that number will increase further to 1,935,000. There are 7.8 million households in the UK that contain 13.6 million children. In 2009 around 90 per cent of them were entitled to claim tax credits and 5.8 million families claimed them. This means that most households with children are drawn into a system that has very high net rates of withdrawal, particularly where it interacts with other benefits such as housing benefit. The result is that many households face the kind of effective marginal tax rates Nigel Lawson ended for high earners when he reduced the top rate of tax to 40 per cent in the 1988 Budget. This does huge damage to work incentives for families with children caught up in these kinds of rates of benefit withdrawal.

The credits have increased labour market attachment by providing an incentive for a person to seek work, because payment of the credit is conditional on a person working a minimum number of 16 hours a week. The withdrawal rates, however, vitiate the incentive to do additional work once a person has a job. The rules that require a person to work a minimum of 16 hours a week in order to claim the working tax credit create perverse results where people arrange only to work the minimum number of hours to qualify for the credit, when their employers would find it convenient if they were to agree to work longer hours. In many workplaces, as the former Labour Minister for Social Security, Frank Field has said, there is little connection between the pay differentials determined in the market that reflect individual workers' marginal revenue products and the post-tax and benefit incomes different employees take home in the same work place.

Other means-tested benefits such as income support, housing benefit and disability living allowance mean that for many individuals, benefits offer a replacement ratio to earnings that either represents a very high portion of their potential earning or in some cases may exceed it. For people of working age this can lead to

Social security transfer payments and age-related spending

permanent detachment from the labour market, particularly if they live in social housing.

The extent and range of social security benefits paid to people of working age needs to be reduced. Both in-work benefits and out-of-work benefits need to be reviewed. The review should include improvements in testing of disability, availability for work and job search. The level of benefits should be looked at from the perspective of both their affordability in public expenditure terms and their impact on labour market incentives. The decision in the Emergency Budget in June 2010 to change the price index used for up-rating social security benefits from the Retail Prices Index to the Consumer Price Index will help in the future.

Saving money and getting a labour market that works

TAX CREDITS NOW ACCOUNT FOR £24 BILLION and spending on them will rise to £28.5 billion in 2015-16. Consideration should be given to significantly reducing their total cost and returning to a system that is closer to the arrangements that existed in 1997. In 1997-98 up-rated for 2010 prices, total help given to families with children was around£14.5 billion:

- Child benefit, £9.6 billion;
- Family credit, £1.5 billion;
- Income support and other child-related benefits, £3.4 billion.

Today a roughly comparable figure would be £35 billion, principally composed of tax credits (£24 billion) and child benefit (£11.4 billion). The £35 billion also includes an element of in-work benefit paid to working households that do not have children. So the figures are not completely comparable. The Coalition's Emergency Budget announced proposals to limit the scope for higher income households to claim tax credits. Households with incomes above circa £30,000, depending on the number of children they have, will no longer be able to claim tax credits, which will save £625 million. This should be seen in the context of other changes that will increase the cost of tax credits as well as increasing the damage done to work incentives. Some £18–£20 billion should be removed from this element of social security spending. Such a change alone would reduce public spending by around 1.3 per cent of GDP. It would be better to have these paid as social security benefits administered nationally by the Department of Work and Pensions rather than the Treasury and HM Revenue and Customs.

The time has come to examine ways of adjusting social benefits for people of working age to take account of regional cost of living indices and local labour market circumstances. Methods of giving local authorities control over the range of social security benefits paid to people of working age should be assessed. The government should consider giving local authorities discretion over housing benefit, jobseeker's allowance, disability living allowance and targeted in-work benefits such as the working families tax credit. The objective should be to ensure that these benefits take much greater account of local area costs and labour market conditions. The principal purpose would be to lower the local benefit replacement ratio. That would also result in further cash savings in terms of the social security budget. Nationally, such changes to tax credits, housing and unemployment benefits should not be cost neutral, but should yield savings of at least two percentage points of GDP, in cash terms around £30 billion from a social security budget of £195 billion.

Britain's long-term social spending challenges

THE UK, LIKE ALMOST ALL ADVANCED OECD ECONOMIES, has an ageing population which will result in increases in government spending on pensions and other age-related areas such as health and long-term care. These issues were explored by Nigel Lawson in a 1984 Green Paper 'The Next Ten Years: Public Expenditure and Taxation into the 1990s'. That Green Paper contributed to the policy discussion that resulted in the UK deciding to reduce significantly the generosity of the second state pension, then called the state earnings-related pension scheme (SERPS). Since then there has been much discussion of how governments in advanced economies will have to finance higher spending when there will be more older people needing assistance and a lower ratio of people of working age to support them. It arises out of the conjunction of three factors: people are living longer; birth rates were lower in the 1970s and social security; and other state spending obligations agreed by governments mainly between the 1940s and 1970s are coming to their full maturity.

In the 1990s economists started to look at the implications of this for future public expenditure and taxation. Led, Jagadeesh Gokhale and Laurence Kotlikoff's paper 'Generational Accounts: A Meaningful Alternative to Deficit Accounting' (1991) developed a framework called generational accounting. What this work exposes is that both the US and most countries in Europe have very large unfunded public expenditure liabilities in addition to their conventional public debt. Moreover, as Alan Auerbach and Ronald Lee explain it in 'Demographic Change and Fiscal Policy' (2001) short-run measures to stabilise government budget deficits 'are grossly inadequate' given 'the true state of fiscal policy'.

The UK government has for some years tried to project the impact of an ageing population on the future level of public expenditure in documents such as the Treasury's long-term public finance report. The Office for Budget Responsibility in its pre-Budget forecast in June 2010 set out its projections of how an ageing population, the retirement of the baby boom generation will increase spending on health, long-term care and the state pensions, with some offsetting reductions in reduced spending on education. Compared with 2009–10, total spending on age-related items will rise by over 2 per cent of GDP by 2029-30, around 3.5 per cent of GDP by 2039–40 and almost 4 per cent of GDP by 2049–50 (see Table 9.1).

Sorry, We Have No Money

	2009–10	2019–20	2029–30	2039–40	2049–50
Health (%)	8.0	8.5	9.3	10.0	10.3
Long-term care (%)	1.2	1.4	1.7	1.9	2.1
Public service pensions (%)	1.8	1.9	1.9	1.8	1.7
State pensions (%)	5.5	5.3	5.9	6.5	6.5
Education (%)	6.0	5.9	6.0	5.8	5.7
Total (%)	22.5	23.0	24.8	26.1	26.3

TABLE 9.1:   *Projections for age-related expenditure (per cent of GDP) (Source: HM Treasury, OBR Pre-Budget Forecast June 2010)*

These projections should, as the Office for Budget Responsibility emphasises, only be regarded as indicative, 'because of the great uncertainty over population projections and the sensitivity to [the] underlying assumptions.' These projections are also based on unchanged policies. It is not, however, clear that the British government will be able to maintain its present policy in relation to certain items of age-related expenditure such as the basic state pension and long-term care.

In some respects the UK appeared better placed to meet these challenges as its policy liabilities in terms of legal commitment are limited. The UK's state pension is a very basic income floor, steps have been taken to equalise and raise the pension age for women and the cost of the state second pension has been cut and the general pension age is being raised. On the other hand, unlike in for example the US, all these liabilities are completely unfunded and work on the basis of pay as you go, essentially financed out of current tax.

The question is, how realistic is this limited present strict legal set of spending obligations in relation to pensions and long-term social care? The national insurance basic pension offers only a very limited income. Moreover, because for many years from 1981 the basic pension was only up-rated in line with RPI price inflation, over time its relative value in relation to earnings fell from around 20 per cent of average earnings in the early 1980s to just under 16 per cent in 2009. It is not clear whether that was ever sustainable.

The last Labour government was increasingly supplementing the basic pension with more generous means-tested pensioner credits and non-means tested winter fuel payments and free television licence fees. In 2007-08 total spending on the basic pension was £47,409 million, on the means-tested pension credit £7,463 million, on non-means tested winter fuel payments £2,071 million, and on TV licence fees £510 million. This meant the basic pension already had to be supplemented by an additional 20 per cent of public spending. The last Labour government had decided to return to up-rating the basic pension by earnings after 2012. The Coalition government's decision to increase the pension by earnings, the CPI or at least 2.5 per cent is a step towards a more realistic policy. While addressing the level of the basic pension is necessary, so is the need to raise the pension age as life expectancy rises. The age at which a person can get their pension has an important influence on labour supply and the government is right to raise it. The precise basic pension age is, however, only one issue as householders over 60 can claim the pension credit and effectively retire early.

Within the UK's social security rules there are several that aim to limit expenditure that has a cruel impact on the lives of vulnerable elderly people. These include withdrawing the basic state pension from people in hospital for longer periods and reducing the pension given to people living in residential and nursing homes with care paid for by the state after a means test to just over £20, which is then supposed to pay for clothes, hairdressers, newspapers and 'treats'. These rules in the longer term will not be sustainable, nor will the present arrangements for the financing of long-term care.

Sorry, We Have No Money

The Coalition government's agreement committed the government to setting up a commission to look at a range of ideas such as a voluntary insurance scheme. Given the limitations of insurance markets, the fundamental issues raised by the Sutherland Royal Commission into long-term care that recommended state funding of care, will have to be revisited. The current position in the UK is perverse. A person can have any amount of trivial medical care for free through the NHS, whereas people with serious acute and chronic personal care needs of the sort that someone requires when they have dementia or have suffered a stroke, receive little or no financial assistance until their assets fall and they are in the hands of the social security system. The issues of the rules surrounding the basic pension and long-term care illustrate an awkward feature of UK public spending. Although it currently absorbs close to 48 per cent of GDP, there are still many things that it should be doing in relation to older people and some other areas of spending that it does not do properly and will be under pressure to increase in the future. There needs to be a significant re-ordering of priorities within public spending.

Accurately measuring the full debt and long-term social security and other care liabilities requires many assumptions. These include judgments about population age, fertility, labour market participation, the proportion of young people in further and higher education, real GDP growth and interest rates. What is apparent from these studies done by the European Commission and the ECB is that the UK may have a much larger stock of future liabilities in relation to GDP than was once thought likely. One study by economists at the IFO Institute identified the US and UK as having the highest level of unfunded liabilities among the countries examined. Christian Hagist, Stefan Moog, Bernd Raffelhüschen and Johannes Vatter in 'Public Debt And Demography – An International Comparison Using Generational Accounting' (2009) concluded that:

> 'the market friendly Anglo-Saxon countries are clearly living their current

lives on credit while Continental Europe has at least achieved some fiscal responsibility with the latest reforms of its welfare states.'

The funding gaps that they identify for the US and UK are very large, 408 per cent for the US and 547 per cent for the UK. The authors acknowledge that this outcome is a surprise. Their forecast for economic growth and their chosen discount rate may be pessimistic, but the whole analysis of generational accounting raises uncomfortable questions about the sustainability of both present levels of taxation and future levels of spending. The IFO study was based on data for 2004, before the credit crunch exposed the full extent of the UK's current problems and before estimates of trend GDP growth were lowered.

While the authors of the IFO paper comment that both the US and UK are better placed than other countries to raise their tax burden, the failure of tax revenue to come through on the scale expected when taxes were raised in the first part of the 2000s, suggests that the UK may be encountering some limit on taxable capacity of the sort that the economist Colin Clark thought existed in the 1940s. In 1945 Clark thought that the realistic peacetime limit on taxable capacity was around 25 per cent of national income. As incomes rise it is reasonable to expect taxable capacity to rise as well, and it may now be around 38 per cent of GDP. This would suggest that pushing up the tax burden further on any significant scale over the coming forty years would be difficult.

Sorry, We Have No Money

Part 2
Capitalism, market limits, state failure and an over-expanded state

Chapter 10: Why markets generally deliver, sometimes fail, and why correcting market failures can create state failure

THIS CHAPTER EXPLORES why the price mechanism is the best way of allocating resources and generally conducting our economic activity. It also explores why markets have limitations, in effect why the creation of large state sectors in the first 60 years of the 20th century yielded clear benefits. And it looks at the imperfections and costs of public intervention and the reasons why we need to be alert to state failure as well as market failure. The issues go to the heart of serious economic analysis. Much of the literature on it is theoretical, technical and difficult. Yet it provides powerful and often simple ideas and assumptions that enable people to analyse all sorts of complex social phenomena.

The market economy is a formidable machine for creating wealth and allocating resources efficiently. It enables innovation, it rewards efficiency and penalises failure. It has its ups and downs, the economic or business cycle will always be with us, but over time capitalism is a remarkable system that enables wealth accumulation to take place and living standards to be raised.

Markets deliver the goods

CAPITALISM'S MOST SUBTLE ANALYST and most persuasive exponent still probably remains Adam Smith. In his book 'The Wealth of Nations', published in 1776, Smith offered the powerful insight that a huge range of devolved decisions taken often for unattractive individual motives of self-interest rather than resulting in disorganised chaos, combine into a co-ordinated and efficient system for giving people the goods and services they need. Far from chaos, economic life is co-ordinated by the 'invisible hand' of the market. Moreover, the success of this system is not dependent on the special virtues of the actors involved, but arises out of the practical 'self-interest' of people doing business. The fact that self-interest, far from being a hindrance, was an incentive that enabled the system to perform without the need for the people involved to be especially altruistic has always been a source of revulsion to many people.

Why markets generally deliver

Yet to recognise that a social system of production can work well without any special virtues on the part of the people involved was great insight on Smith's part. As Sir Samuel Brittan, the *Financial Times*'s distinguished economic commentator, has pointed out, just because a system can function well on the basis of self-interest and is not dependent on altruism does not mean that generosity and the virtues of altruism in any way undermine the system and have to be avoided. Indeed many of the most successful early modern capitalist business families were Quakers. They were not only generous in their personal charity, but often prospered in their business, because they were trusted by their customers for their honesty. John Mueller has pointed out in 'Capitalism Democracy and Ralph's Pretty Good Grocery' that it was said that a child could be sent to buy something from a Quaker tradesman, and would not be cheated and would return with the right change. This did not always result in the customers acknowledging the inherent integrity of their Quaker business community. Rather it was sometimes said that the Quakers were only honest because it was good for business. Yet as Brittan argues the system could function without virtue, but that does not mean that people were not virtuous. That is a great strength for a social system, because virtue with a capital V is often in short supply particularly where there are arguments over money or resource allocation within a community.

Private vices, public virtues and Mandeville's notorious paradox

SEVERAL OF THE EARLY ECONOMIC THINKERS in the 17th and 18th centuries were medical doctors. Among them are Sir William Petty, John Locke and the French economist Quesnay. One Dutch doctor living in London, Dr Bernard Mandeville a generation before Adam Smith, achieved a huge *succès de scandale*, with the publication of a book titled 'The Fable of the Bees, or Private Vices Public

Benefits' in 1714. In his British Academy lecture on Mandeville in the academy's master mind series in 1966, F A Hayek explained how even after over 250 years Mandeville was not quite reputable. In Mandeville's *Fable*, the bees one day are smitten with virtue. They turn from sinful pride and enjoyment of luxury to virtue. Whereas pomp pride and vanity created employment and prosperity, when the bees became virtuous, frugality produced a slump. *The Fable of the Bees* shows how virtuous behaviour could in effect be punished and licentious conduct be richly rewarded. In Hayek's words Mandeville became 'a bogeyman, a name with which to frighten the godly and respectable, an author whom one might read in secret to enjoy a paradox, but whom everybody knew to be a monster by whose ideas one must not get infected.'

Mandeville contrasted the difference between the selfishness of the motives of people and the benefits which the resulting actions conferred on others. Mandeville's central argument was that the complex order of society results from actions that very often produce different results from those that had been principally intended. In short, individuals pursuing their own ends and purposes whether for selfish or altruistic reasons produced useful results for others. Mandeville had set out in Hayek's judgment for the 'first time the classical paradigmata of the spontaneous growth of orderly social structures: of law and morals, the market and of money, and also of the growth of technical knowledge.' Although many people were plainly 'infected' by Mandeville's paradox, Adam Smith himself went out of his way to reject Mandeville. Smith classed *The Fable of the Bees* as a 'licentious system' and attacked him in 'The Theory of Moral Sentiments' published in 1759. It is widely recognised that Mandeville's scandal made possible modern social theory and cleared the way to the philosophical frame work of David Hume and the Scottish Enlightenment that Smith himself drew on. There is no doubt that Mandeville's paradox has continued to fascinate economists ever since. Lord Keynes greatly admired Mandeville and called on his analysis when developing his own theories of consumption. Joan Robinson was likewise drawn to *The Fable of the Bees* which she explored in her book 'Economic Philosophy: An Essay on the Progress of Economic Thought' (1962). While Hayek recognises that Mandeville was the first person to coin the term 'division of labour' and did much to clarify that phenomenon, Hayek does not rate Mandeville as a technical economist in the way that Keynes did, rather dismissing him as a mercantilist. Yet in Hayek's judgment Mandeville's paradox set out in *The Fable of the Bees* intellectually cleared the way for David Hume and Adam Smith and classical political economy.

Markets need rules

WHAT BOTH SMITH AND BEFORE HIM MANDEVILLE recognised was that markets broadly left to their own devices without government regulation and interference were the best way of organising economic life. Individual decisions combine spontaneously to produce order. Moreover, well-intentioned attempts to interfere or meddle with those private decisions through policy and legislation or to divert and interrupt the flow of benefits that spontaneously come from them will damage society as a whole. For Mandeville and Smith government intervention and direction of economic activity damages trade and prosperity. That does not mean that markets and capitalism can flourish in a vacuum of social anarchy where there are no state or community institutions. Far from it; governments have to establish the rules of the game and frameworks of legislation for the proper conduct of business.

Generations of modern economists have recognised the importance of a proper legal framework. The rule of law and government institutions are a necessary condition for capitalism and its markets to work. Economists, however, probably did not fully appreciate the importance of the rule of law and reliable government institutions until the collapse of Communism and the challenges faced by the transition economies of Central and Eastern Europe over the last twenty years. And for many contemporary economists the amount of intellectual effort and interest that Hayek put into thinking about markets in the context of law and frameworks of legislation which he set out in his book 'Law, Legislation and Liberty' (1973-79), was something of a puzzle. Yet the fundamental challenge of getting that basic framework of legal institutions right was fully exposed in the practical struggles that the transition economies had in establishing the rule of law. An independent and competent judiciary is necessary for the enforcement of contract and the protection of property rights are necessary conditions for markets, while effective competition rules and insolvency procedures are needed if markets are to work efficiently. This is a hugely important job for government.

Whereas twenty years ago most policy makers would have seen them as principally challenges for transition economies and developing economies, today it is plain that these complex issues present real challenges for advanced economies. The accountancy scandal exposed by Enron and other company scandals have shown that there are huge issues of corporate governance and trust that go to the very heart of the rules that are needed to make modern markets work. The issues exposed in the tech wreck, the Enron fiasco and the credit crunch expose huge flaws in the procedures that are supposed to ensure that the firms and joint stock companies in particular are transparent and honest entities in the sense that the Quaker businesses acquired their reputations for probity. In modern economies senior managers at the heart of businesses appropriate resources to themselves in a manner that should not happen. The agency problems that arise out of the separation of the ownership and control or management of businesses have been shown to be real matters for direct concern, whereas once they were generally regarded as merely interesting subjects for academics and confined to the seminar room. The guardians of capitalism's financial integrity, moreover, the accountants, auditors, actuaries, lawyers and credit rating agencies, have failed to carry out their duties in any common sense understanding of their responsibilities.

Why markets generally deliver

So in setting the rules for the game governments have a big job on their hands. In the contemporary context a great deal needs to be done to address the clear and continuing systematic failures in corporate governance. The need for significant improvement in corporate governance goes far beyond banking and financial services regulation – the whole structure of corporate governance and the fundamentals of accounting and auditing need to be improved.

Capitalism remains the only show in town

DESPITE THE HUGE DAMAGE done by the credit crunch and the recognition that many of the ground rules that markets need have not worked, capitalism remains the only show in town. In September 2008 just after the collapse of Lehman Brothers, the Archbishop of Canterbury Dr Rowan Williams interestingly suggested that Karl Marx was right after all. Dr Williams attacked greed and expressed a revulsion against capitalism and individualism with a spontaneous vigour absent from his usual modus operandi that suggested that his revulsion was not simply provoked by the banking crisis. In attacking the market economy Dr Williams was both reflecting and tapping into a general mood that the time for liberal markets was over and there should be a return to a more collectivist if not planned approach to economic life. In fairness to Dr Williams he was careful not to offer any kind of detailed agenda, other than to suggest that there should be better financial market regulation. Yet it was plain where his moral compass was directing not just him but his advice to the rest of us. On the issue of whether Marx was right Dr Williams is simply mistaken. Far from being right, Marx was fundamentally wrong. Marx vividly explored the way that capitalism allocates resources and enables dramatic accumulations of capital to take place through a system that rewards success and penalises failure and ruthlessly clears away failure. That process is unstable. The process of accumulation is periodically interrupted; that economic or business cycle, however, leads to steadily rising living standards for the great majority of people. Marx sets out the power and vigour of capitalism's creative destruction and how in the process it accumulates huge wealth as well as any economic writer, but that was not his special and distinctive contribution to economic argument. Marx's novel suggestion was that at some stage capitalism would exhaust all its profitable opportunities and that after one final bout of accumulation, it would fall into a state of permanent depression where most people would endure a condition of general misery.

This simply has not happened.

Even when capitalism has gone through serious periods of crisis such as the Great Depression, living standards remained much higher than they had been a generation before. A J P Taylor, the Oxford historian and socialist polemicist, set out the position as clearly as anyone writing about the interwar years. In his 'English History, 1914-45' published in 1965, Taylor explained how in the 1930s, while unemployment was a curse for the individuals and communities touched by it, the great majority of people were in work and although money wages fell by 3 per cent, because prices fell, real living standards rose by 10 per cent. In Taylor's judgment:

'those in work, and there were always more of them, were better off than they had ever been. Hence the problem of unemployment, though formidable as statistics and terrible of course for those that endured it, remained strangely remote from the mass community.'

The interesting thing to note about Taylor's conclusions is that they were made before the extensive revisionist economic histories of Britain's economic performance in the 1930s were written. Sydney Pollard has shown in 'The Development of the British Economy, 1914-80' (1983) that real working class income rose by over 30 per cent in real terms between early years of the 20th century and the mid to late 1930s. Derek Aldcroft in articles such as 'Economic Growth in Britain in the Inter-War Years: A Reassessment' in the *Economic History Review* (1967) showed that not only was the British economy growing faster than before 1914 but important structural and technical changes took place that were of vital significance for

Why markets generally deliver

the future long-term growth of the economy. This work of revision has significantly modified the received folk memory of unqualified economic distress and generalised falling standards of living during that period. Understandably the vivid folk memories maintained by images of the Jarrow marchers and the literary achievement of Walter Greenwood's novel 'Love on the Dole' (1933) have made a greater impression on people such as Dr Williams than the statistical analysis that informed Alan Taylor's judgment.

Today an essentially lightly regulated liberal economy remains the principal way most policy makers and political parties see the future. President Obama has by American standards a 'liberal' or left wing agenda on things such as health care and trade union rights, but the President has no interest in any kind of planned or regulated economy. In the UK there is no suggestion that there should be a return to the mixed economy of the kind that Britain had from the 1940s to the 1980s. The return to social democrat policy reflexes expected by many people during the acute crisis in 2008 and 2009 does not appear to be happening. Capitalism across the world has lifted millions of people out of poverty in China and India. It remains the recognised instrument for dynamic accumulation of wealth and income. Instead there is an important agenda about ensuring that the system works in a more reliably stable, fairer and honest manner in the interests of the public as a whole. An important part of that agenda and debate is to ensure that certain economic agents in the system do not appropriate resources that ought to belong to other people. These include bankers, company directors and senior public sector managers. These economic rent seeking agents are able to acquire inappropriate income and wealth because of an imperfect set of incentives and institutional arrangements.

Sorry, We Have No Money

Chapter 11: The neo-classical analytical paradigm

IN GENERAL, RESOURCES SHOULD BE ALLOCATED through freely operating markets. Yet in modern successful economies there is extensive state intervention and departure from the price mechanism and as Vito Tanzi and Ludger Schuknecht have shown, public sectors that are large by historical standards have resulted in significant improvements in economic and social welfare. One of the best books written on the role, costs and limits of the public sector is David Heald's 'Public Expenditure: Its Defence and Reform' (1983).

The reason why this literature is difficult is that economists have tried to be more precise in constructing their arguments and have increasingly used formal mathematical models to improve the logical consistency of their arguments. Stephen LeRoy, a visiting scholar at the Federal Reserve Bank of San Francisco, has put it very well in a research note 'Is the "Invisible Hand" Still Relevant?' (May 2010). Economists have abandoned the informal and elegant literary style of Adam Smith for the refinements of precision.

This chapter draws heavily on David Heald's summary of this extensive literature. Heald starts from different set of biases from me. He wrote the book from the perspective of an economist attached to the post-war Keynesian social democratic approach to the welfare state. As well as being an academic economist he has stood for Parliament as a Labour candidate. Heald provides an exceptionally lucid and comprehensive survey of the rationale for market pricing, its limitations and potential policy remedies. He also provides a cogent exploration of the extensive literature on why those remedies can be disappointing in their results as a consequence of state or collective failure.

The starting point for any serious analysis is the recognition that resources are scarce and are given value in relation to their relative scarcity. As a result they need to be used properly and used efficiently. The best mechanism for doing this is the price mechanism. Prices, as the economist William Stanley Jevons famously demonstrated when he solved the diamond-water paradox, are determined by

The neo-classical analytical paradigm

relative scarcity[1]. The neo-classical framework that emerged out of the so-called marginalist revolution in economics in the 1870s has provided us with a powerful set of analytical tools to look at these issues. The cornerstone of this analysis is the notion of marginal utility or happiness and the fact that utility diminishes at the margin more as something is consumed. Not only does utility diminish at the margin but so do costs and returns. Normally firms will produce goods and sell them at a price where the marginal cost of production equals the marginal revenue that they receive. Firms are profit maximisers and that is the point where they maximise those profits.

Within this neo-classical framework there are a series of assumptions. All economic agents are rational and have perfect information. Markets are efficient. Products are homogenous; firms are price takers rather price makers. There is perfect competition, there are many competing firms and many consumers and firms that freely enter and exit a market, allowing production and prices to adjust freely. These are highly stylised assumptions that offer useful abstract tools for analysis. These assumptions do not describe the real world, they are only helpful abstractions for analysis. The neo-classical framework is a static analysis based around exacting standards of rigour that make analysis difficult; dynamic competitive markets exhibiting high levels of entrepreneurship are difficult to study not least because the exacting conditions for properly functioning markets will rarely be present. Yet the crude intellectual tools of the neo-classical tradition continue to offer the best starting point for much economic analysis. Indeed the last forty years have seen the intrusion of economic analysis into all sorts of areas of social analysis and public policy that might have been considered immune from the attentions of economists. These areas have ranged

---

1   The diamond-water paradox arises out of relative prices - water is essential for life yet costs little to consume compared to diamonds that are unnecessary to life but cost a fortune.

Sorry, We Have No Money

from the arts and sex and race discrimination to criminal behaviour and education and training.

Conditions for Paretian optimality

WITHIN THIS NEO-CLASSICAL PARADIGM across the economy resources are optimally distributed if welfare or utility cannot be improved for any one individual without another individual suffering some loss of welfare as a result of the re-arrangement. This is called Pareto optimality and is named after the economist who identified the conditions for the best or optimal distribution of resources within the neo-classical apparatus of economic analysis. Vilfredo Pareto set this out in his book 'Manual of Political Economy' in 1906. This concept of Paretian optimality is at the heart of modern welfare economics and cost benefit analysis. It assumes individuals maximise their personal welfare, that they are rational and that they are the best judge of their own welfare. And it assumes the decisions can be made rationally and objectively and separated out from other social, psychological and political considerations and are in that sense objective. This framework of analysis has a strong presumption in favour of individual decision making and action as opposed to collectivist state action. Pareto in effect reformulated Adam Smith's arguments in favour of private competitive markets. Pareto offers a refinement and a more precise formulation of Smith's approach and a set of criteria to assess how efficiently resources are being allocated.

There are three dimensions to Paretian optimality: exchange efficiency, technical efficiency and overall Paretian efficiency. Exchange efficiency is about making sure that a combination of consumption goods is allocated between individuals to ensure changes cannot improve the position of one person without making another worse off. The marginal rate of substitution measures a consumer's willingness to give up one good in exchange for another. Where this is equal for all consumers, so no further reallocations are possible

The neo-classical analytical paradigm

that satisfy the condition that no one should be made worse off, exchange efficiency is established. A similar analysis establishes the conditions for technical efficiency in the production of goods. The optimal combination of factors of production is where the marginal rate of substitution between any two factors of production is equal for all goods that are produced. When this condition is met it is not possible to reallocate factors of production so that more of one good is produced without producing less of another good. The optimal composition of output as a whole is overall Paretian efficiency. This is reached where the marginal rates of substitution coincide so that both production and consumption are aligned so that no further changes can be made to make one person better off without making another person worse off. There is no single allocation of resources that alone meets the conditions for Paretian optimality. Instead there are a range of such allocations that correspond to different distributions of welfare, which in turn reflects on different initial factor endowments which is the starting point for trade and market transactions between economic agents.

The efficiency presumption against public expenditure

A DEPARTURE FROM ALLOCATING GOODS THROUGH PRICES is a departure from Paretian optimality. If governments provide goods free of charge the result is that consumers will continue to wish to consume them and they will be provided even when the marginal benefits of the additional consumption is lower than the marginal cost of producing the good or service. In that sense government expenditure normally implies a loss of welfare and efficiency unless there are special factors in play. The over-consumption and production of goods and services that fails to take account of the marginal utility or benefits that it generates is the principal efficiency objection to public expenditure and the public provision of goods and services that ought normally to be produced in the market using the normal price mechanism. This is the core argument against the

government providing goods and services either free or at heavily
subsidised prices at the point of delivery.

X-efficiency

In the standard neo-classical economic framework when the
various conditions for allocative efficiency are in place the assumption of profit maximisation guarantees that firms will produce their
output at the minimum attainable cost. In the 1960s and 1970s
this profit maximisation and cost minimise assumption about firms
came under increasing scrutiny from an American economist working at Harvard University, Harvey Leibenstein. Leibenstein set this
work out in a series of articles starting with 'Allocative efficiency vs.
X-efficiency' in the *American Economic Review* in 1966 and 'Beyond
Economic Man: A New Foundation for Microeconomics' in 1976.
He argued that economists worried too much about the losses of
economic welfare generated by distortions such as monopoly being small compared with the losses of welfare that result from firms
using more inputs to produce a given level output than was necessary. Leibenstein coined the term X-efficiency to describe these
losses of economic welfare. Leibenstein explained that these losses
of X-efficiency often arose out of the fact that firms failed to adopt
new methods of production and techniques of best practice. The
extent of X-inefficiency is the difference between the maximum
effectiveness of using all the inputs of labour capital and land and
their actual use. Allocative efficiency will not be achieved unless all
X-efficiency has been achieved. Leibenstein made the point that
economists simply assume that full profit maximisation is taking
place within the firm and then go on to explore other matters such
as allocative efficiency. Leibenstein suggested that microeconomists
should go to greater efforts to explore the internal operations of
the firm rather external matters such as competition and market
structures. External pressure from market competition constrains
the degree of X-inefficiency and that constraint is obviously absent

in the circumstance of market concentration or monopoly. Although Leibenstein's work was an important contribution to the theory of the firm it perhaps had even greater implications for public sector output that takes place in the absence of competition or effective challenge.

Governments have to intervene in the economy because the highly stylised assumptions of the neo-classical framework do not prevail in practice. Markets are not perfectly competitive, products are not homogenous. There are barriers to entry that prevent firms from setting up and entering a market. The fact that markets are not perfectly competitive or that firms have a degree of market pricing power in the highly stylised manner of the neo-classical analytical framework does not mean that markets do not work reasonably efficiently or that market capitalism is not the best way of allocating resources efficiently and producing goods and services. But it makes plain that governments will have to intervene to correct the behaviour of markets and those interventions will go beyond a simple framework of rules for contract and accounting. Governments have to have effective competition policies. And governments have to intervene to correct markets where the prices do not fully capture the economic costs and benefits involved in activities. This means that there are market failures that have to be corrected by government intervention and there are limitations on what markets can in practice offer, particularly insurance markets. These market failures and limitations are the reason why government intervention and collective action can yield genuine benefits. They explain why the expansion of government activity in the 20th century in advanced economies from about 13 per cent of national income in 1913 to around 33 per cent in the mid 1960s yielded so many identifiable benefits.

Sorry, We Have No Money

Externalities, market failure and public goods

THE PRINCIPAL SOURCE OF MARKET FAILURE arises out of marginal costs not fully capturing the cost to the wider community of producing a product or service. These are usually referred to as externalities. The firm does not incur the cost and because it is a cost that the firm does not face neither does the consumer. This can result in an excessive production of a good where its true or full marginal cost is greater than the marginal benefits it is producing. The classic example of such a market failure where costs are not fully captured by ordinary pricing is environmental pollution. These issues were first seriously explored by a Cambridge economist Arthur Pigou in his book 'The Economics of Welfare' published in 1920 where he used the compelling example of the smoky chimney[2] to illustrate his point about externalities. As well as negative costs being generated by production that are not captured by market prices in the usual way there can also be positive or beneficial effects arising out of production that may not be fully captured by the price mechanism. These positive externalities can be identified in areas such as education, health and housing.

Paretian economics presented a powerful and compelling case for the use of markets and prices in allocating resources, but it also provided an intellectually rigorous basis for much public sector intervention to correct market failure. The presence of negative and positive externalities implies that firms and individuals being left narrowly to pursue their self-interest will not result in an economically or socially optimal allocation of resources. Pigou, for example, suggested that there should be taxes and subsidies to modify the decisions that firms and individuals made. Socially optimal output

2   While neighbours will have to bear the costs that arise out of the smoke from a factory chimney, such as washing that has to be rewashed, buildings that suffer acid damage from soot deposited on walls and the consequences of the smoke in terms of disease and poor health, the company will not. The company that owns the factory will sell its products without having to take account of the full cost of their production.

The neo-classical analytical paradigm

requires production to be expanded through subsidy until the marginal benefit of socially beneficial goods equals the marginal cost of producing them. This does not in any way lead to the automatic conclusion that there should be extensive public ownership or direct public provision of goods and services through public spending at no cost or price to the consumer. The acknowledgement of the existence of externalities does, however, sanction extensive state or public intervention, provided that the benefits from such public action exceed the costs.

The recognition of externalities within Paretian welfare analysis takes the case for public intervention much further than the simple provision of so-called public goods. Classic public goods such as defence and lighthouses represent a much narrower category of goods and services than those that would be justified by the correction of market externalities. Paul Samuelson in the 1950s offered what has become a widely accepted definition of a public good and it is quite specific or narrow. The two main conditions are:

❑ There is non-rivalry in consumption so that one person's consumption does not reduce the amount available for others; and

❑ It should be impossible to exclude benefit from a person who refuses to contribute to the cost.

A public good does not have to be directly produced by the state. It could just as well be produced by the private sector and financed by the state. Samuelson's analysis also pointed to the fact that many economic activities had the character of public goods and an economy without a public sector would not be achieving its optimal level of output.

Apart from the refinements of externalities within neo-classical economic analysis there is also an older justification for public intervention that arises from the concept of consumer surplus. This idea was developed by French engineer Jules Dupuit in the 1840s. Consumer surplus arises from the consumers' willingness to pay for a service relative to the amount of benefit received. In certain circumstances where the marginal and average operating cost of providing a service are zero, charging for it will result in costs to the consumers. Consumers will use it less than the full social benefits would warrant in the absence of charging. Dupuit was a highway engineer and developed consumer surplus into a sophisticated argument against tolls on bridges and roads. The same efficiency arguments can be applied to other public facilities which exhibit low or very low marginal costs once the decision to provide the facility has been taken. Such facilities include public parks, open spaces, beaches and museums. These should on efficiency grounds be free with no charges until demand is high in relation to capacity so that congestion has to be managed. Prices involve transaction and the use of resources costs. The abolition of a toll removes a cost from the operator of the bridge, but there are other costs such as the time incurred by travellers and the costs that arise out of travellers arranging their journeys to avoid the toll. Market rationing through prices involves costs and those costs can exceed the costs of the rationing arrangements put in place by the private sector. These long-standing arguments that arise out of the concept of consumer surplus suggest that the use of prices will not always lead to allocative efficiency and the institutional framework in which they are being applied has to be closely examined.

Asymmetries of information, adverse selection, moral hazard and limitations of insurance markets

THERE ARE MANY RISKS in life that can have devastating consequences for individuals and their families. These range from motor accidents to premature death, illness, and theft and fire from the home. Since the 18th century insurance markets have developed to deal with these risks and in many instances they work well at a reasonable cost. There are some risks such as the risk of premature death and house fires that insurers have been able to work out and cost with relative ease since the 18th century. Yet there are many risks that insurers find difficult to calculate and will only provide at great expense or with exclusions that effectively vitiate the policy when a person tries to claim against it.

Insurers face practical difficulties when they offer insurance products for things such as incomes in retirement, unemployment cover, health cover, or mortgage protection if a person loses their job. Most of the modern work done on these difficulties was done by Joseph Stiglitz in the 1970s. He identified two problems that insurance companies face - asymmetry of information and adverse selection. They are essentially simple but powerful ideas. The insurance company and the person being insured do not possess the same amount of information. The person may be a very healthy person who comes from a family that enjoys good health and lives to a great age. The insurance company does not really know that much about the individual so it has to assume something worse than the average. That pushes the cost up for everyone, including below average and average risks. There is then the issue of adverse selection. People seeking to insure risks probably think that they are potentially exposed to them. In some areas of risk such as fire the risks are less likely to be very precise to the individual but other risks such as health risks or litigation risk may well be more specific to the person seeking the insurance protection. So the people mostly likely to need to claim on the insurance policy are the kind of people who take out the insurance protection. And once people have taken out the protection there is moral hazard. People have a tendency to claim, partly because they believe they have less need to be prudent in their behaviour on the principle of 'well, it is insured'.

These issues of asymmetry of information, adverse selection and moral hazard place limitations on the role that insurance markets can play in the economy. There are many risks that individuals face that insurance markets cannot deal with at a reasonable cost for many households. This is why frameworks of social insurance of one sort of another have been developed in most advanced OECD economies. They cover many of the things that traditional insurance tried to provide at a high price to the limited number of households that could afford it, for example provision of income for individuals of working age who cannot work as the result of unemployment either through economic dislocation, temporary illness or permanent disability, and health cover and income in retirement during old age. In recent years private insurance markets have found it difficult to offer households reliable and cost-effective help with long-term savings for old age through insurance pension arrangements.

State failure and public sector inefficiency

WHERE THERE IS A NEED for public goods or to correct market failure or simply remedy the limitations of the price mechanism there is a strong presumption that supports collective action of one sort or another. Correcting a market failure or stepping in with a collectivist solution where there is a market limitation does not always result in a better allocation of resources. As governments in advanced economies expanded their reach during the middle and second half of the 20th century it became apparent that there could be state as well as market failures. Identifying market failure in terms of Paretian optimality is one thing, identifying effective remedies and designing policy instruments at a reasonable cost is another. The use of taxes, subsidies and establishment spending programmes results in other costly externalities. Successful state intervention to remedy market failure requires there to be altruistic public policy makers who maximise social welfare untainted by the motivation of specific sectional political interest or indeed self-interest. Not only must policy makers be altruistic they must be omniscient, possessing full information about costs demand and skilled in the use of the framework of analysis offered by Paretian welfare analysis.

The Paretian framework is generally perceived as a liberal market framework that relies on relative prices to allocate resources. Shortly after Pareto published his book one of his students, Enrico Barone, published an article in 1908 that demonstrated that while marginal cost pricing and perfect competition may be necessary to achieve Paretian optimality, private ownership of the means of production may not be necessary. Barone's implication was that socialist planners could achieve Paretian efficiency by operating theoretical or shadow prices. Elizabeth Durbin in 'New Jerusalems: The Labour Party and the Economics of Democratic Socialism' (Routledge & Kegan Paul 1985) summarised the position of socialist economists in the middle of the 20th century. 'The new socialist economics used existing microeconomic theory to spell out the economic tasks which a collective system would have to perform in order to allocate resources efficiently.' H M Treasury book 'Microeconomic Reform in Britain: Delivering Opportunities for All' (2004) offered a contemporary economic analysis by the Government Economic Service rooted in that tradition of identifying market failure and using government policy to remedy it. For example, it saw taxation as the way to promote productivity and growth positive externalities. The aim of policy was 'to strengthen markets where they work in the public interest, to tackle market failures where they occur whilst recognising that there are some areas where markets are not appropriate and where market failure can only be dealt with through public funding or provision of key services'. It went on to argue that 'when a market is inappropriate, policy design must set out to how to avoid the trap of simply replacing market failure with state failure.' The Treasury argued that 'a more decentralised system that matches the attainment of ambitious national standards with the promotion of local autonomy can shape both efficiency and equity'. It is ironic that the book should perceive public policy making at that time as an exercise in decentralisation given the detailed national targets that so shaped and distorted public services. It is also interesting that the book simply asserts that equity, efficiency and national targets and local autonomy are consistent and complimentary and appears oblivious to the fundamental tensions

Sorry, We Have No Money

that potentially play between them. It is not surprising that some economists who would perceive themselves as liberal supporters of market economies have become critical of the application of the Paretian framework and its impact on policy. Sir Alan Peacock in 'Economic Analysis of Government and Related Themes' (1979), for example, refused to accept that Paretianism will consistently result in liberal non-authoritarian solutions to problems of economic policy.

The same challenges that confront a full socialist planner confront policy makers identifying market failure within the neo-classical framework. Many of the economists most interested in welfare economics and correcting market failure were democratic socialists. Prominent among them were Evan Durban, Arthur Pigou and Abba Lerner. Their central problem was lack of information. They often were attracted to using devices such as shadow prices and internal markets to create the information that would normally be offered by the conventional price mechanism. There is no doubt that the British economic establishment has been heavily influenced by this approach. Treasury officials and the Government Economic Service have possessed the ready reflex of identifying market failure and the need for public intervention to correct it in the same way that Treasury officials were most comfortable when pursuing hair shirt policies that involved reining in either present or future consumption by individuals and households. Nigel Lawson recognised this intuitive austerity on the part of Treasury officials and jokingly called it 'Crippsian'. He put it down to a Treasury legacy associated with the post-war 'rigid austerity' Labour Chancellor of the Exchequer Sir Stafford Cripps. I always saw it as a kind of entrenched Fabian cast of mind dressed up in the rigorous clothes of Paretian optimality and neo-classical economic rationale.

This was always most evident to me when I worked at the Treasury and saw the response of officials to the public expenditure statement that was for many years set out in the autumn and the tax policies set out in the spring budget. Each spring a discussion

The neo-classical analytical paradigm

of some minor net reduction of total tax revenue of £1–3 billion would be greeted by Treasury officials with much sucking on lemons and a lot of worry about fiscal irresponsibility. While each autumn tens of billions of pounds would be added to public expenditure with barely a hint of concern about the probity of the public finances. In my opinion this radical asymmetry in the response to the consequences for budget arithmetic of a tax cut compared to higher spending illustrated this fundamental Fabian collectivist outlook.

In the second half of the 20th century as the range of government activity and intervention expanded it became apparent that government generated its own welfare losses and suboptimal outcomes. In short the decision making process that led to public sector intervention was not omniscient or altruistic. Decisions about collective action and government spending were not made by the kind of public spirited guardian envisaged by Plato. Instead there is an imperfect decision making process that reflects complex economic, social and political incentives. And the combination of imperfect information and vested interests in government bureaucracies resulted in resource allocation that while intending to correct imperfections in the market resulted in significant costs that could lead to damaging and malign results.

The first economist to address seriously the issues of potential state failure was James Buchanan. Buchanan's starting point is that Paretian welfare economics is an open system that exposes market failures yet treats the potential remedies available in state action as exogenous. In a properly closed system of analysis, market failures would be compared to state action which would be examined and its weaknesses and perverse outcome would also be exposed. Buchanan argued that before any firm conclusion can be reached about the role of the state, as well as measuring the costs of market failure the consequences and cost of state failure have to be recognised. Buchanan's work led to the creation of the public choice school of economic analysis that looked at the interaction between economics and the political process. Economists such as Gordon Tullock and Richard Wagner along with Buchanan exposed the economic consequences of an imperfect political process. The heart of this analysis is that they combine consequences of vote seeking politicians, supported by budget maximising bureaucrats, which create the conditions for not only particular examples of state failure, but also potentially for an over-expansion of the public sector budget as a whole in modern democracies.

There is a fundamental challenge of finding a democratic political mechanism for allocating resources efficiently. It is very difficult to produce an aggregate set of choices that represents the genuine aggregation of individual preferences. Kenneth Arrow showed how difficult it would be to construct a set of procedures for making public decisions that consistently and accurately reflect individual preferences and that it is impossible to construct a set of social orderings of preference that reflect individual choices. Expressed at its simplest, collective action arrangements that are intended to maximise a social welfare function based on individual choices or values cannot do so with consistently unambiguous results. In short, it is impossible for public policy decision makers to know.

Over-expansion of the state

LEAVING ASIDE THE PRACTICAL DIFFICULTY of knowing what social welfare is, there is no reason to assume that public officials whether elected or unelected would chose to maximise it. In 1957 Anthony Downs published 'An Economic Theory of Democracy'. In seeking to explain the behaviour of politicians in a two-party democracy, Downs assumed that political parties would seek the support of voters in the middle to maximise their vote. Yet he noted politicians were also utility maximisers and that their utility function included ideology and the chances of getting re-elected which constrained their pursuit of the median voter's social welfare. A similar application of economic theory of the firm to the

The neo-classical analytical paradigm

behaviour of bureaucracies was made by William Niskanen in 'Bureaucracy and Representative Government' (1971).

The picture that emerges is of political decision making that distorts decisions in two separate ways. The first is the distortion between the voter and the elected politician. The second is the distortion created by the relationship between politician and bureaucrat.

The first distortion, the imperfect connection between voter and politician gives rise in the judgment of Buchanan and Tullock to the over-expansion of the public sector because of asymmetries about the costs and benefits of the expenditure and taxes involved. The benefits of public spending tend to be overestimated while its costs are underestimated. The benefits of spending are canvassed by interest groups that advocate particular areas of spending. There is no comparable mobilisation on behalf of taxpayers who will foot the bill, because the burden of spending is spread among all taxpayers. This approach was challenged head on by Downs. He argued that while certain items of expenditure might be over-expanded through this mechanism, because the benefits of public expenditure are diffuse whereas individuals are acutely aware of the taxes they pay, as voters they are reluctant to sanction higher spending. J K Galbraith in the late 1950s vividly captured Down's judgment coining the famous aphorism 'private affluence and public squalor'. It is difficult objectively to test either judgment.

The second distortion that arises is between the interaction of the elected politician and bureaucrat. In William Niskanen's application of economic theory to bureaucracy, the relationship between politician and bureaucrat is best analysed as a 'bilateral monopoly' in which the politician is the sole supplier of money and the bureau is the sole provider of output which the politician values. The bureau's output is not marketed. The absence of market valuation makes it exceptionally difficult to monitor. The politician will not have a reliable or confident knowledge of the cost involved and must infer output levels from the bureau's level of activity as measured by the physical inputs into the total budget. This results in an opaque environment where significant goal displacement can take place. The salary and prerequisites of the office, public reputation, patronage and convenience and ease of managing the service may well displace the explicit set goal or purpose of the organisation.

Rising real unit cost of public expenditure: Baumol's disease

GROWTH IN PUBLIC SPENDING has reflected not just an expansion of state activity but an increase in its cost. In the 1960s William Baumol observed that many of the services that the expanding public sector provides offer fewer opportunities to reduce costs over time. Indeed Baumol argued that there may be a relative price effect that actually results in the costs rising. Some areas of public spending offer little or no scope for efficiency improvements in unit costs. He distinguished between activities that were technologically progressive where economies of scale, capital accumulation and technical innovation result in cumulative increases in output per person and activities where these were not present and there is little likelihood of output increasing per person. Baumol's notion of public sector relative prices turns on differences in their inherent technology, not of other things that can be modified such as value for money. In the context of steady long-term economic growth and real living standards increasing, the unit costs of the non-technologically progressive sector will increase relative to those of the progressive sector. This is because both sectors will have to compete for employees in the same labour markets and trade union pressure will oblige public sector employers in the medium term to maintain pay comparability with the progressive sector. Baumol regarded a progressive increase in the ratio of public spending to national income as inevitable. Increasing externalities requiring government intervention to improve resource allocation and income distribution would lead to an explosion of public expenditure and unbalanced

The neo-classical analytical paradigm

growth where the ratio of public spending rises within GDP. This
is often referred to as 'Baumol's disease'. The main activities where
these factors are in play are personal public services such as personal
social services where there is a close and often intimate connection
between the quantity of labour used and the quantity and quality
of service provided. An arresting example of the non-progressive
character of certain activities is that of the performing arts. However great the improvement in labour productivity since their first
performances, there remains the same number of parts in an Ibsen
play or Schubert trio. A publicly financed production of a play or
concert will need the same number of actors or musicians as was
needed a hundred years before.

Public sector X-inefficiency

LIEBENSTEIN'S WORK ON X-efficiency was originally an exploration of the internal dynamics of the private sector corporation or
firm. The notion of X-inefficiency, however, has enjoyed a much
wider understanding and application in relation to the public sector. There are good reasons to doubt that the relative cost effect of
the public sector is simply explained in terms of barriers to growth
in productivity arising out of technology. Public expenditure is
more likely to exhibit losses of X-efficiency than the private sector, because of the absence of appropriate internal incentives. This
is obviously the case given that there is no profit maximiser with a
claim on the residual savings that can be made after X-inefficiencies
are eliminated. Therefore no one has an effective incentive to save
costs.

Leibenstein emphasised from the start that competition both actual and potential has a critical role in containing X-inefficiency.
Public sector output that is not marketed is obviously much less
exposed to competition. There is neither the profit motive nor the
threat of bankruptcy in the public sector. In 1983 David Head asked
the pertinent question of whether in the non-market public sector

it was possible to use alternative mechanisms to expose and drive out X-inefficiency. Heald had in mind mechanisms such as external scrutiny, budgetary stress or a simple commitment to a public service ethos of public service efficiency. Since the early 1980s many attempts have been made to introduce these sorts of mechanism. There is now within the public sector the risk of institutional reorganisation, and in that sense institutional death. Whether it improves efficiency is not clear, because institutional death in the public sector is very different from that in the private sector. In practice it creates opportunities for additional losses of X-efficiency through the working out of redundancy, early retirement and the creation of new, re-graded and higher-paid public sector jobs. Losses of X-efficiency in the public sector are, in addition to the distortion and losses of economic welfare that arise out of allocating resources, outside the framework of marginal cost pricing that is at the herat of the Paretian paradigm. As Heald neatly puts it: 'more extensive X-inefficiency is therefore piled upon allocative inefficiency'. Loss of X-efficiency is therefore a kind of double blow to efficiency in the public sector, analogous to the double taxation of savings under an income tax system.

William Niskanen applied the X-efficiency analytical framework to the public sector and concluded that it was more X-inefficient than the private sector, because it did not have the same disciplines and internal incentives. Given that there is no profit motive, there is no one with an incentive to claim savings that are made by rooting out waste and seeking X-efficiency.

These problems are not simply confined to the public sector but also extend to other non-market sectors such as foundations, churches and voluntary organisations. They affect all organisations that receive all or part of their revenue other than from the sale of marketed output. There are broad types of non-market that can be considered sources of X-inefficiency. These are internal and private goals. In non-market settings these goals and objectives are removed from the discipline of the market and instead depend

The neo-classical analytical paradigm

upon the self-discipline of those running the organisations. Goals other than maximising the cost-effectiveness of the organisation may be selected, such as pioneering technical advance even when it is economically unviable. Redundant and rising costs occur in circumstances where output is difficult to define and measure; the monitoring of costs may be defective, with the result that there are redundant costs and a tendency for real costs to increase over time. Derived externalities are unpredicted side effects of public sector bodies that impose additional costs on both public sector and private sector organisations, with the result that new programmes are introduced to rectify the damage done by existing public sector programmes. Distributional inequity arises where equity and economic welfare can be breached not just by market mechanisms but by the non-market sector as well.

Competing bureaucracy, privatisation, contracting and contested public sector markets

WILLIAM NISKANEN'S APPLICATION of the X-efficiency framework of analysis suggested that the private sector may be more X-efficient than the public sector. Significant savings could therefore be made by contracting out and privatising public sector functions. The broad implication of the extensive literature that developed on these issues in the 1970s and early 1980s was that the production of public services should be contracted out. There should be privatisation, contracting out and tendering. The common theme running through this literature was the need for competition, real or stimulated. Public provision and public sector costs should be contested and interrogated. Public sector bureaucrats should be given personal financial incentives to maximise cost savings, such as allowing the retention of a proportion of these savings. US literature explored the benefits of competing bureaucracy, something that naturally interested US economists given the overlapping range of both Federal government agencies and the interaction between state and federal government agencies. What this literature did not fully address was the important but separate set of issues relating to whether introducing competition into the production and provision of public services will be sufficient to overcome the fundamental challenge that politicians and civil servants still have to commission the service and will use tax revenue to finance it. Would these attempts to create contested public sector markets overcome the inherent challenges of economic distortion, perverse incentives and the malign consequences of the deadweight effects of the taxation necessary to provide the revenue to finance the contracts? Someone has to commission the contracts and appropriate money to pay for them. A market-contested private sector may merely transfer the point at which state failure comes into play. Contracting out may merely change the framework or mechanism that generates X-inefficiency.

The key issue about state failure is that it obliges policy makers arguing for public intervention to correct market failure to recognise that identifying a market failure or imperfection is not sufficient to justify public intervention to rectify it. A market failure has to be matched by an effective remedy. And public sector remedies may impose their own direct economic distortions and failures that arise out of chronic cost inefficiencies. Where public expenditure is involved in addition to any conventional distortion in terms of the neo-classical framework, perverse and unintended consequences and the losses of X-efficiency, the cash spent will have to be raised from taxation. Taxation itself imposes a further deadweight cost on the economy that distorts economic behaviour and results in slower growth in national income in the long term.

The neo-classical analytical paradigm

Chapter 12: Sweden and the Nordic model

THE NORDIC MODEL has been held up as an example of how high levels of government spending can be maintained alongside successful free enterprise and high living standards. It is often used as the counter-factual to the widespread evidence from the research literature that shows that beyond a certain level, a high ratio of public spending to national income slows growth of GDP and living standards. Mary Hilson, who has found much to admire in the Scandinavian social democrat welfare model, shows in her book 'The Nordic Model: Scandinavia Since 1945' (2008), that much myth surrounds its alleged economic success and explores how it has come under pressure. The myth that Hilson identifies can be roughly summarised as follows. Until the 1930s the Scandinavian countries were poor and backward economies in the north west of Europe that suffered badly in the Great Depression. In response to the inter-war crisis, in Sweden, a Red–Green coalition government of social democrat and agricultural farmers' parties took office in 1932. It abandoned orthodox liberal policy in the early 1930s and secured as a result a spectacular recovery in output that then set the stage for a golden age of economic advance and welfare services in the 1950s and 1960s.

Hilson shows how Sweden, in particular, had caught the attention of democratic socialists in the 1930s. The pathway was identified in 1936 by the American journalist Marquis Childs in 'Sweden: the Middle Way' (1936) that used Sweden as an example of how, in Scandinavia, compromise could be reached between freedom, market capitalism and a form of extensive corporatism and social security and Childs contrasted it with fascist and communist responses to similar problems. The British Labour politician and economist Hugh Dalton in the preface to Brinley Thomas's 'Monetary Policy and Crises: A Study of Swedish Experience' (1936) described the Swedish recovery as 'sensational' and hailed it as nothing less than 'an economic miracle'. The Nordic model has remained since then both an inspiration to the left and a counter-factual to the

Sweden and the Nordic model

accumulating literature about an over-expanded public sector in OECD countries.

Mary Hilson explains that much of the encomia given to the success of the Swedish model are overdone, if not a myth. Sweden in the inter-war years behaved like other small open economies. In common with the other Nordic countries it had developed a large export sector because of its limited domestic market, and historically this was based on raw materials which Scandinavian countries had in abundance – iron ore, tar, timber, furs, pulp and paper. In the inter-war years Sweden's economy behaved in the way that a small export-dependent economy would be expected to behave given what was happening to the rest of the world. By 1900 the Scandinavian countries were well integrated into the North Atlantic and European economies. The First World War resulted in a speculative boom in commodity prices. In the early 1920s Sweden had a serious inflation problem and then experienced rising unemployment as commodity prices fell, culminating in the Great Depression. In the second half of the 1930s Sweden experienced a strong recovery in output led by its export markets. The Swedish economic recovery in the 1930s was principally due to structural factors and favourable export markets in particular, rather than to innovative counter-cyclical policies pursued to stimulate domestic demand. In the 1940s Sweden benefited economically from being neutral in the Second World War. Its economy was helped by increased trade with Germany. In the late 1940s and 1950s it benefited from American Marshall Aid in common with most of the Nordic countries and its exports benefited from the recovery in western Europe that was partly stimulated by the Marshall Aid transfers.

Mary Hilson makes the point that modern economic historians attribute much of the improvement in the performance of the Swedish economy between the 1930s and 1950s to these structural issues, rather than attributing it to any distinctive Swedish policy model. Hilson also draws attention to the fact that with the exception of Finland, Nordic growth rates were generally below the

Sorry, We Have No Money

OECD average. This was particularly marked in the 1950s when GDP growth was 1–1.5 percentage points lower. Hilson's judgment is: 'clearly, then, some important structural reasons account for Scandinavian economic performance during the golden age. Given the position of the Nordic countries as open economies able to benefit from favourable condition in the rest of Europe, it might be expected that economic policy would have less impact.'

To the extent that Sweden established distinctive economic policies and institutions to support them, the question has to be asked how well such arrangements would travel to other political communities. The Swedish model was based on an economic agenda presented by two economists, Rudolf Meidner and Gosta Rehn, to Sweden's trade unions in 1951. The Meidner-Rehn model was an institutional adaptation of standard Keynesian demand management to contain the inflation that it was already causing, while maintaining high levels of employment. There were four dimensions to the model: a wages policy; the stimulation of saving and a public investment policy; a liberal trade policy based on private enterprise; and active labour market polices. In many respects, these were approaches that were later to be used by non-Nordic economies such as the UK when the Keynesian welfare model started to break down and progressively higher and unstable levels of inflation started to emerge in the 1960s and 1970s. Countries increasingly turned to wages polices to contain inflation and had to employ direct price controls to achieve consent for their incomes policies that then distorted and seriously damaged resource allocation.

Sweden was unusually well placed to reach agreement on a long-term plan for wages. It had both powerful and highly centralised trade unions and comparable employer organisations. This meant both sides could reach agreement and make the bargain stick. This was the result of being a small and homogenous political community with a distinct history. Such social arrangements are difficult to construct in societies where there is not a similar shared political consensus. Even in Sweden it started to break down in the late

Sweden and the Nordic model

1960s, when miners at a state-owned company in Lapland staged a wildcat strike in 1969.

In the 1970s and 1980s, as Sweden's terms of trade deteriorated and its export markets were less buoyant the public sector expanded as an employer of last resort. State subsidies to production prevented and delayed necessary industrial restructuring and stored up problems for the 1990s. Sweden's spending on education, training and research was high, but the results were poor. The OECD in regular reports catalogued very low economic rates of return on research and development, education and training. High marginal tax rates vitiated the incentive to acquire human capital because the after-tax rate of return was too low. While many commentators continued to hail the Swedish model and exemplified in particular its record on research, training and education, rigorous international scrutiny was showing that these were disappointing in their results. I based a note for John Major, when he was Chancellor of the Exchequer, on this literature from the OECD and called it 'Sweden: A Paradise Lost'.

In the 1990s the Swedish model that had been exhibiting strain since the 1970s, for all practical purposes broke down. There was a deep recession, a huge increase in unemployment and an acute fiscal crisis. The fiscal crisis was so acute that its management is now part of the international literature on how government debt and deficits should be brought down, and was referred to in the UK's Emergency Budget in June 2010.

The Swedish crisis was part of a broader problem in the Scandinavian model. Niels Ploug, in 'Denmark – Conditions of Life – The Scandinavian Welfare Model' (2004), a paper for the Royal Danish Ministry of Foreign Affairs, shows how many of the elements of the Nordic welfare model expanded and developed in the 1960s and 1970s. When these additional elements were introduced economic growth was robust and unemployment was low. Moreover, it was never 'the intention either with unemployment, sickness benefits or with cash benefits that so many people should receive them or that they should receive them for so long as there has been the case in recent years.' Ploug's judgment is that 'the financing of the welfare state has thus become a problem, and as it has not been politically possible to increase taxes, which are already very high, the Scandinavian countries have accrued a very large national debt which on the long view could represent a threat to the welfare systems.'

The Nordic model does not offer a contradiction of the broader international research that suggests that after a certain point there is a connection between high levels of public spending and disappointing economic performance. Instead, it illustrates how there is not some kind of mechanical formula. Economic growth will be influenced by a whole range of factors, from the structure of export markets and natural endowments of raw materials to broad cultural traditions such as a work ethic embodied in the Lutheran tradition. Market economies need to be open to trade and integrated into the international economy. They also need a fundamental framework of rules, regulation and law. The Nordic countries benefited from being integrated into the world economy and from stable property rights and the rule of law. James Gwartney, an American economist who has done a lot of work on both the role of public spending in slowing economic growth and the role of legal institutions, recognised in his Presidential address to the Southern Economic Association in 2008 that Nordic countries by being open to trade, and protecting property rights and maintaining the rule of law, sustained living standards, despite higher public spending. In amongst all these other factors, however, an expanded public sector beyond a certain point will retard economic performance.

There are many things to admire about Sweden and its Scandinavian neighbours in the 20th century. Not least the maintenance of democratic institutions, personal freedom and levels of prosperity. The success attributed to the Swedish model, however, has been exaggerated and it has not endured. Assar Lindbeck in 'Swedish Lessons for Post-Socialist Countries'(1998), pointed out that public spending in Sweden did not reach the OECD average until 1960, when the ratio got to 31 per cent of GDP. In 1950 it was still only 25 per cent. In the period before the First World War Sweden outperformed comparable advanced European economies. That out-performance increased between 1913 and 1950, a period punctuated by two world wars where there was strong demand for raw materials at a time when Sweden was neutral and able to maintain increased trade with its closest trading partners and Germany in particular. Between 1950 and 1973 Swedish growth accelerated, but was around a fifth lower than in the other comparable economies. In the thirty years to 2003 the rate of growth significantly diminished in Sweden and in the other comparable economies but Swedish growth remained below that of the others. When the economic crisis hit Sweden in the early 1990s, unemployment increased sharply, from 3 per cent or less before 1991 to 9.4 per cent in 1994. Unemployment then remained high for almost a decade. In the recent slump in international output Swedish GDP contracted by around 6 percentage points, more than the OECD average of just over 4 per cent. Unemployment in Sweden rose to 8.3 per cent in 2009 compared to 7.6 per cent in the UK.

The OECD country report on Sweden in 2008 makes the point that in 1970 Swedish GDP per capita was less than 10 per cent lower than in the US. However, after the deep crisis in the 1990s GDP per capita fell to a level around 25 per cent lower than in the US. Until the recent economic crisis the gap had started to narrow as market-orientated reforms boosted productivity and the attractiveness of work increased. The OECD's judgment is that the combination of high public spending and taxation combined with rigid labour market policies created an institutional framework that had 'weakened the economy's ability to adjust' as the initial rise in unemployment was followed by a persistent rise in the share of working age adults living on unemployment benefits.

The OECD report also notes that educational outcomes are not as good as they used to be and that the PISA educational proficiency measures show Sweden to be above average in terms of literacy but not for maths and science teaching. Moreover, during the period of robust economic expansion between 2005 and 2007 youth unemployment remained high, falling from 22.8 per cent to 19.2 per cent, despite buoyant economic activity. Intergenerational earnings mobility in Sweden is weaker than in OECD countries such as Australia, Canada and other Nordic countries. The OECD suggests that 'this might indicate that the extensive redistribution of income has not necessarily increased equality of opportunity.'

It is difficult to sustain the case that Sweden and the Nordic model more generally contradict the broader evidence about the manner in which public spending after a certain point crowds out future economic growth and retards the evolution of national income.

Conclusion

THE UK, IN COMMON with most advanced OECD economies, developed an extensive public sector when it created the modern welfare state in the 1940s. That resulted in a much higher level of public expenditure than economies normally exhibited in peacetime. Moreover, this larger public sector yielded genuine and identifiable benefits. However, there is a cost to public spending and it is higher than just the cash cost of the actual spending. That cost arises out of the distortion that both public spending and taxation creates in the economy and results in a less efficient use of resources, the so-called deadweight cost. It is therefore important that spending at the margin results in benefits that are greater than its full economic cost.

At some point in the 1960s the UK economy appears to have passed the point where higher spending yields obvious benefits and does little apparent damage. The 1976 White Paper on public expenditure graphically set out the consequences of a rising tax burden that requires taxes to be levied on people with incomes that are considerably lower than average earnings. Robert Bacon and Walter Eltis in their book 'Britain's Economic Problem: Too Few Producers' (1976) showed how an expanding public sector that has to be paid for by taxes imposed on the private sector eventually undermines the private sector's capacity to pay the taxes that are needed. In their estimate, the UK probably passed that position in the early 1960s. They also showed how an expansion of public spending beyond a certain point creates a structural problem that eventually has to be dealt with, even if that overexpansion takes place in context of low inflation and general financial stability.

Vito Tanzi and Ludger Schuknecht have demonstrated the genuine benefits of having a much larger public sector than was historically the case. They have also illustrated the damage that is done economically when public spending increases beyond the point where it yields returns greater than its full costs. Most economies should be able to accomplish all that they need to do with a level of public spending no greater than 35 per cent of GDP. The UK

Conclusion

needs to lower its ratio of public spending from close to 48 per cent of GDP to 35 per cent of GDP. As a general rule of thumb, over the economic cycle public spending should be kept to that level. That means in recessions it may be higher and in booms it should be lower.

There is a substantial body of research that has looked at these structural public expenditure issues. This suggests that beyond a 'certain point increased public spending slows the growth of economies and private sector consumption. It is probably a mistake to be too mechanistic about it but the higher spending reduces countries' growth rates from what they would otherwise have been. If countries have a lower level of public expenditure, over time the evolution of real GDP per capita will be greater and that will eventually finance higher real levels of public services, in the sense that a lower ratio of spending in terms of a much higher level national income is worth more than a high ratio of public spending in an economy where national income is much smaller.

The critical matter is the total level of public expenditure. How a given level of public spending is financed between taxation and borrowing is a secondary matter. The borrowing merely represents deferred taxation. Once borrowing and the stock of government debt are above a certain level, government deficits become a public expenditure issue in their own right. Regular large deficits and high levels of government debt also make the management of monetary policy more difficult for the central bank. That is the position that the UK and US are now in. The discretionary increases in taxation and reductions in spending announced by the previous Labour government in the March 2010 Budget and by the Coalition government in the June 2010 Emergency Budget are necessary. Over six years, if these measures are implemented in full, they will reduce the budget deficit to just over 1 per cent of GDP and will reduce public spending to just under 40 per cent of GDP. This will resolve the UK government's borrowing problem but is insufficient to deal with its medium and longer-term structural public expenditure problems.

Market economies work best when there is a proper framework of conduct for their operation, to enforce contract, competition and corporate governance. In general, most decisions about the allocation of resources are best left to the market. There are, however, limitations in the way that markets work. Over time, the market economy or capitalism has yielded huge benefits. It is unstable and distinguished by periods of over-accumulation, which are then followed by periods of contraction. Over time it generates higher incomes and wealth that raises the living standard of the great mass of people. Attempts to move to either fully planned economies or mixed economies with a significant socialised and planned element have had disappointing results. Despite the recent banking crisis and the Second Great Contraction in the world economy, the market economy offers the only practical way forward. However, a great deal needs to be done to improve corporate governance, banking and financial regulation, as well as the conduct of the guardians of a market economy's rules, the accountants, lawyers and credit rating agencies.

The full benefits and costs of many activities are not fully captured in market prices. There are obvious areas where markets fail and have to be corrected. Insurance markets exhibit genuine limitations so that there are many important risks that can only be properly and efficiently managed through collective public action and expenditure. The market economy results in wide dispersions of income that many political communities choose to modify on grounds of social equity, but also to avoid the practical costs of living with neighbours and communities that are impoverished and the cause of wider social problems and tensions. From the time of Tudor England, Parliament has legislated to relieve poverty. These market failures and limitations are the reason why the expansion of government action in the first sixty years of the 20th century yielded such clear benefits.

Conclusion

Market limitations and failures point to the need for public intervention and the collective provision of many goods and services. Yet market failure has to be balanced with consideration of state failure. There is a central public sector efficiency problem that arises out of allocating resources outside the price mechanism and through political and bureaucratic procedures where there are fewer penalties for failure, less financial discipline and bankruptcy is largely absent. When someone else is paying for a good or service the recipient has no reason to worry about cost or over-provision of the service. The managers of public services have few effective incentives to control their budgets and to spend taxpayers' money optimally. There are losses of X-efficiency in the private sector. In the public sector these losses are greater than in the private sector, because there is nobody who benefits from financial savings that result from increased efficiency. The reflex is one of 'it's in the budget' or 'it has been through a process'. The interaction of raw politics, a lack of bureaucratic incentives to control costs, and powerful producer interest groups combines to result in an over-expansion of public spending.

Over the last thirty years the UK has tried a succession of reform and management innovations to address the inefficiency of public sector spending. These include: cash limits, efficiency scrutiny of spending, contracting out, the creation of the Audit Commission, the creation of government agencies, devolving budgets to schools, an internal market in the health service, the citizen's charter, the private finance initiative, accruals accounting, public service agreements and increasing use of quasi markets, contestability, challenge and the money follows the client. Many are worthwhile and have yielded benefits. Despite all these measures, the fundamental deficiencies that limit the public sector's incentive to manage public money efficiently have not been remedied. Indeed, the process where 'change is the only constant' may have actually aggravated some of the public sector's management deficiencies. The lesson is

Sorry, We Have No Money

that there are no simple technical or managerial solutions that will make the public sector more efficient or productive.

This unpalatable truth is demonstrated by looking at the results of the huge increase in real resources in the public sector after 1997. Increased spending has not been matched by comparable increased measurable outcomes. The extensive analysis done by the ONS shows that between 1997 and 2007 productivity in the public sector fell. Moreover, that fall in productivity is estimated after a special inquiry by Sir Tony Atkinson, that made some upward adjustment to take account of quality. Some public sector organisations, such as the Audit Commission challenge the ONS's measures of output on the grounds that they do not fully capture improvements in quality. The ONS work, however, appears to be consistent with the wider debate about the efficacy and outcomes of increased public spending that has taken place in recent years. The National Audit Office and Public Accounts Committee reports on hospital doctors' pay, the GP out-of-hours service, maths teaching in primary schools, adult numeracy and literacy education, the Sure Start programme and the public-private partnership for the modernisation of the London Underground tell a story that is consistent with the ONS's findings. When the Public Accounts Committee looked at resource management across government departments in 2008 it found that there is some way to go 'before financial management is fully embedded within departmental cultures and given the priority required for services to be delivered efficiently and cost-effectively'. The report, 'Managing financial resources to deliver better public services', found that only 41 per cent of departments' policy proposals always included a full financial appraisal and only 20 per cent of them based policy decisions on a thorough assessment of their financial implication. There would have to be some extraordinarily imaginative delivery of service if such poor financial management could be compensated for by improvements in quality that match the losses of productivity implied by the ONS work. There is no clear evidence to suggest that the UK public sector is any more

Conclusion

efficient or able to achieve efficient results from its use of public money than it was thirty years ago.

The heart of the UK's public spending problem in terms of its relative lack of efficiency and productivity is an entrenched public sector producer interest. The only part of the UK economy that remains significantly unionised is the public sector. Close to 60 per cent of public sector employees are members of a union. The only part of the economy where there is a significant identifiable trade union mark-up or wage premium is the public sector. Management in the public sector over the last twenty years has lacked confidence and been reluctant to address pay, staff performance, attendance and absence through sickness. Median average weekly earnings in the public sector are over 12 per cent higher than in the private sector. While arguments can be made about the composition of the public and private sector workforces, it is difficult to avoid the conclusion that many employees in the public sector are both paid more than would be justified by any notion of an efficiency wage and more than a practical sense of affordability would suggest. Public sector pensions take the overall compensation matter a stage further; public sector pension arrangements mean that public sector employees enjoy a deferred wage premium of 12 per cent compared to private sector employees. To correct this, public sector pay and pensions should be reduced by at least 17 per cent, which in cash terms would yield a saving of around £30 billion, or just over 2 per cent of GDP.

The social security benefits such as income support, housing benefits, working tax credits and disability living allowance create both unemployment traps and poverty traps. These work to permanently detach many individuals and households of working age from participation in the labour market. They create poverty traps that blunt the work incentives of millions of people recorded as being in work. The average replacement ratio of social security benefits to earnings has changed little from the 1970s, when it was 60 per cent, to today, when it is around 56 per cent. Spending on

Sorry, We Have No Money

social security transfer payment on people of working age needs to be reduced by at least £30 billion. Lower benefits compared to wages will not just save money but will increase the incentive to take work by lowering the replacement ratio of benefits relative to wages.

The UK has a significant regional economic problem. There are many communities and whole regions that have become detached from effective participation in the international market economy. An expanded public sector with high wages paid at nationally agreed terms and conditions means that the going rate of pay in many communities is above the average marginal revenue product for the locality. This contributes to an unrealistic local reservation wage that is further entrenched by an effective floor to wages that results from social security payments set at national rates that take little or no account of local labour market circumstances. The combination of national social security benefits, national rates of pay for the public sector and an expanded public sector has been to create regions dependent on transfer payments. In these local economies the labour market is emasculated and relative prices do not operate. As old industrial and traditional industries declined, the local economy could not adjust because an expanded public sector overrode the operation of the market signals needed to bring the adjustment about. The public sector instead further crowded out the remaining and weakened private sector. A similar process took place in the East German regions that formed the old GDR. The UK has as a result of the way it managed de-industrialisation and ignored the supply performance consequences of a large public sector produced not just de-industrialised, but de-marketised communities and regions.

The issue of de-marketised communities should be addressed directly. Public sector pay should no longer be settled nationally. Instead, employers should agree individual contracts of employment with each employee in each workplace with the freedom to adjust terms and conditions to local circumstances. Social security

Conclusion

benefits paid to people of working age should reflect the local labour market where people are looking for work. Local authorities should be given responsibility for paying and managing social security benefits for people of working age in their locality. Councils should be free to experiment with different benefit structures related to an obligation to pursue active labour markets policies locally. Within such a devolution of benefits policy, local authorities should be given an incentive to make savings to ensure that the replacement ratio of benefits to earnings is lower than it is now and reflects local market-based earnings. The principle that local authorities are centrally funded largely through grants to deliver a roughly comparable level of public service throughout the country should be relaxed. Funding of authorities should take greater account of local costs and local gross value added per capita – GDP per capita. Lower funding should be given to communities that should in principle have a lower cost base. In return, as local councils stimulate local employment and businesses they should be given effective tax powers to benefit from their success in expanding their local private sectors.

Simply reducing public spending by the amount necessary to stabilise the budget deficit is a necessary, but not sufficient policy objective. In the 1980s and 1990s the Conservative governments of Margaret Thatcher and John Major stabilised the public finances and reduced inflation, but they made much less progress in resolving the structural public expenditure problems created in the early and mid-1960s, the consequences of which were set out in the 1976 public expenditure White Paper. From the 1970s public expenditure was brought down from close to 48 per cent of national income to around 40 per cent. The performance of the economy was not as good as might have been expected given the scale of denationalisation and labour market reform. The reason for this was that many of the core structural problems that prevented the economy from working properly were entrenched by the level of public expenditure and the tax burden needed to finance it. It is

Sorry, We Have No Money

significant that the average benefits replacement ratio only fell from 60 per cent to 56 per cent. In practice, the tax wedge for many average and low income workers was little changed. And the tax burden continued to descend a long way down the income distribution in the way that the 1976 White Paper described.

While the public sector has been subjected to an extensive managerial reform agenda over the last thirty years, the central producer interests have been left in place. Some of the reform agenda was introduced to step aside from directly confronting those producer interests. Public sector employees, paid through national collective bargaining along with national social security benefit rates, created the conditions for the de-marketisation of communities and regions. This process of de-marketisation was already apparent in the 1990s. Its reversal will not take place without a broader set of policies to make the public sector less expensive, more flexible and more locally focused and controlled. The UK's de-marketised regional problem will not be addressed without a coherent agenda to improve the working of the economy that allows relative prices in regional labour markets to assert themselves.

If the UK is to meet the challenges of the next forty years it will have to improve its supply performance. The proportion of national income that it spends through the public sector will have to fall if that is to happen. Reform of public sector pay bargaining, the reduction in the level of public sector pay and pensions, lower social security transfer payments, a rebalancing of regional public spending and transfer payments and a general reduction in public sector spending should all form part of a coherent approach to improving the supply performance of the UK economy.

This is a difficult, but necessary public agenda. It is based on a realistic assessment of what can be afforded and what will yield benefits in excess of its costs. The UK's public spending challenge is made more difficult because what needs to be confronted are entrenched producer and regional interests in relation to public sector pay, pensions and social security transfer payments. In many respects

Conclusion

the easy public sector reform decisions such as ending consumption and production subsidies and returning the nationalised industries to the private sector were taken in the 1980s. The remaining agenda is about affordably financing spending on publicly provided health, education and social care. The agenda is not about the public sector withdrawing from these areas, but the more difficult one of financing them on a realistic basis and trying to overcome the inherent inefficiencies that public sector provision results in. The UK public sector spending agenda is also difficult because it will involve not just reducing spending as a share of national income but re-ordering spending priorities. With an ageing population the UK will have to spend more on health care for older people, but it will also have to provide more realistic basic pensions and long-term care as well.

The message of this book, however, is an optimist agenda to reform the public sector and lower public spending in relation to national income. From the analysis presented here it is plain that a large public sector yields significant benefits. The UK can afford to spend around 35 per cent of national income on public services in the same way that Australia and Switzerland do and the UK did in the mid-1960s. The Coalition government has already shown how it plans to reduce public spending from almost 48 per cent to just under 40 per cent of GDP. Taking some further radical, but in principle, manageable steps to reduce public sector pay and pensions and to lower social security transfer payments to people of working age would yield more than an additional 4 percentage points of public expenditure savings. In principle, such an adjustment should be possible.

Moreover, as public spending starts to fall, as a ratio of national income, the performance of the economy will start to improve. Lowering the ratio of public expenditure to 35 per cent of GDP is principally about improving the performance of the economy in the medium and long term. There can be pleasant supply performance surprises that raise economic activity and growth as well as adverse surprises. It is possible that as progress is made with an agenda of lower public spending, making regional labour markets more responsive and lowering the social security replacement ratio, the economy will begin to exhibit examples of 'crowding in', where economic growth begins to accelerate at a slightly faster sustainable rate. That would be a bonus; the real prize would be a wealthier economy with higher living standards and an economy better placed to meet the challenges of an older community in a more competitive world over the next forty years.

Conclusion

Bibliography

2009 Annual Survey of Hours and Earnings, November 2009 Statistical Bulletin, ONS

Aldercroft, D. (1967) 'Economic Growth in Britain in the Inter-War Years', *Economic History Review*

Arthur, J. 'Trade Union Membership 2009', BIS ONS

Auerbach, A., Gokhale, J. and Kotlikoff, L. (1991) 'Generational Accounts: A Meaningful Alternative to Deficit Reduction in 1991', Cambridge, Mass., National Bureau for Economic Research

Auerbach, A. and Lee, R. (2001) 'Demographic Change and Fiscal Policy', Cambridge, CUP

Bach, S., Givan, K. and Forth, J. (200) 'The Public Sector in Transition', in 'The Evolution of the Modern Workplace', Brown, W. et al (eds), Cambridge, CUP

Bacon, R. and Eltis, W. (1976) 'Britain's Economic Problem: Too Few Producers', London, MacMillan

Bacon, R. and Eltis, W. (1996) 'Britain's Economic Problem Revisited', London, Macmillan

Bagehot, W. (1867) 'The English Constitution', new edition (2001) Oxford Paperbacks

Bakhs, H., Haldane, A. and Heath, N. 'Quantifying some benefits of price stability', Bank of England Quarterly Bulletin, August 1997

Baratt, C. 'Trade Union Membership 2008', BERR ONS

Barnett, C. (1986) 'The Audit of War', London, Macmillan

Barnett, C. (1995) 'The Lost Victory British Dreams, British Realities 1945-1950', London, Macmillan

Barro, R. (1997) 'Determinants of Economic Growth: A Cross Empirical Country Study, Cambridge, Mass., MIT Press

Barro, R. (1994) 'Are government bonds net wealth', _Journal of Political Economy_

Bell, G. and Tawara, N, (2009) 'The Size of Government and US-European Differences in Economic Performance', IMF

Bevan, A. (1952) 'In Place of Fear', London, William Heinemann Ltd

Brittan, S. (1995) 'Capitalism With A Human Face', London, Edward Elgar

Borensztein, E. and Panizza, U. (2008) 'The Cost of Sovereign Default', IMF Working Paper

Campbell-Smith, D. (2008) 'Follow the Money: The Audit Commission, Public Money and the Management of Public Services, 1983-2008' London, Allen Lane

Carter, A. (1968) 'The English Public Debt in the Eighteenth Century', London, The Historical Association

Cecchetti, S., Moharty, M.S. and Zampoli, F. 'The Future of Public Debt: Prospects and Implications', BIS Conference Paper for Reserve Bank of India's International Research Conference Challenges to Central Banking in the context of Financial Crisis, February 2010.

Clarke, P. 'Churchill's Economic Ideas, 1900-1930' in Blake, R. and Louis, W. R, (eds), (1993) 'Churchill', Oxford, OUP

Dickson, P. G. M. (1967) 'The Financial Revolution in England: a Study in the Development of Public Credit in England 1689-1756', London, Macmillan

Downs, A. (1957) 'An Economic Theory of Democracy', New York, Harper & Brothers

Durbin, E. (1985) 'New Jerusalems: The Labour Party and the Economics of Democratic Socialism', London, Routledge & Kegan Paul

Erdem, E. and Glyn, A. (2001) 'Job deficits in the UK regions', Oxford Bulletin of Economics and Statistics

European Commission Spring Forecast, May 2010

Feinstein, C. H., Temin, P., and Toniolo, G. (2008) 'The World Economy between the Wars' , Oxford, OUP

Financial Statement and Budget Report, March 2010

Glyn, A. and Sutcliffe, B. (1972) 'British Capitalism, Workers and the Profits Squeeze' , London, Penguin Books Ltd

Hagist, C., Moog, S., Raffelshuschen, B. and Vatter, J. (2009) in 'Public Debt and Demography – a Comparison Using Generation Accounting', CESifo DCE Report 4

Hale, D. 'Labour disputes in 2009', *Economic and Labour Market Review*, June 2010

Hayek, F.A. (1973) ' Law, Legislation and Liberty', London, Routledge & Kegan Paul

Heald, D. (1983) 'Public Expenditure: its Defence and Reform' Oxford, Martin Robertson

Heath, A. and Smith, D. B (2006) 'At a Price: the True Cost of Public Spending', London, Politeia

Hilson, M. (2008) 'The Nordic Model: Scandinavia Since 1945', London, Reakton Books

H M Government Green Paper 'The Next Ten Years: Public Expenditure and Taxation into the 1990s' 1984 Cmnd

H M Treasury (2004) 'Microeconomic Reform in Britain: Delivering Opportunities for All', London, Palgrave

H M Treasury Budget 2010 June 2010 HC 61

HM Treasury (2010) 'Debt and reserves management report 2010-11'

House of Lords Select Committee on Economic Affairs 'Private Finance Projects and Off-balance Sheet Debt 2010', HL Papers 63-1

Household Expenditure and Income Tax Rebates of 200, *American Economic Review* (vol. 96, No 5, December 2006)

IMF World Economic Outlook, October 2008

IMF World Economic Outlook Supplement, November 2008

IMF Fiscal Monitor May 2010

IMF (2010) 'Strategies for Fiscal Consolidation in the Post-Crisis World'

Institute for Fiscal Studies, 'The IFS Green Budget 2010', IFS

Kettl, D. (2000) 'The Global Public Management Revolution' Washington, Brookings Institution

Keynes, J. M. (1925) 'The Economic Consequences of Mr. Churchill', London, Hogarth Press

Keynes, J. M. (1936) 'The General Theory of Employment, Interest and Money', Cambridge, CUP

Lawson, N. (1992) 'The View from No 11', London, Bantam Press

Lawson, N. and Bruce-Gardyne, J. (1976) 'The Power Game: An examination of decision-making in Government', London, MacMillan

Leduc, S. 'Fighting Downturns with Fiscal Policy', *FRBSF Economic Letter*, June 2009

Leibenstein, H. (1966) 'Allocative Efficiency and X-efficiency', *American Economic Review*

Sorry, We Have No Money

Leibenstein, H. (1976) 'Beyond Economic Man: A New Foundation for Microeconomics, New York, Harvard University Press

LeRoy, S. (2010) 'Is the Invisible Hand Still Relevant?', Federal Reserve Bank of San Francisco

Lerner, A. (1943) 'Functional Finance and Federal Debt', Social Research

Luengnaruemitchai, P. and Schadler, S. (2007) 'Do Economists' and Financial Markets' Perspectives on the New Members of the EU differ?', IMF Working Paper

Maddison, A. (2007) 'Contours of The World Economy, 1-2030 AD Essays in Macro- Economic History', Oxford, OUP

Mandeville, B. (1714) 'Fable of the Bees, or Private Vices, Public Benefits'

Mayhew, K. et al (2006) 'From Skills Miracle to Productivity Miracle – not as easy as it sounds', *Oxford Review of Economic Policy*

Merkl, C. and Snower, D. (2006) 'The Caring Hand That Cripples: The East German Labour Market After Unification', Kiel Institute

Mouré, K. (1991) 'Managing the Franc Poincaré: Economic Understanding and Political Constraint in Monetary Policy 1928-36' Cambridge, CUP

Mueller, J. (2001) 'Capitalism, Democracy and Ralph's Pretty Good Grocery, New York, Princeton University Press

Niskanen, W. (1971) 'Bureaucracy and Representative Government', Chicago, Aldine-Atherton

OECD Economic Outlook No 87, May 2010

Office for Budget Responsibility' Pre-Budget Forecast', June 2010

Pareto, V. (1906) 'Manual of Political Economy'

Peacock, A. (1979) 'The Economic Analysis of Government', London, Martin Robertson

Pigou, A. (1920) 'The Economics of Welfare', London, Macmillan

Pliatzky, L. (1982) 'Getting and Spending: Public Expenditure, Employment and Inflation' Oxford, Blackwell

Ploug, N. 'Denmark Conditions of Life: The Scandinavian Welfare Model', Royal Danish Ministry of Foreign Affairs

Pollard, S. (1983) 'The Development of the British Economy, 1914-80', London, Edward Arnold

Public Accounts Committee 'Pay Modernisation: a New Contract for NHS Consultants in England 2007', HC 506

Public Accounts Committee 'The Provision of Out of Hours Care in England 2007', HC 360

Public Accounts Committee 'Sure Start Children's Centres 2007', HC 261

Public Accounts Committee 'Skills for Life: Progress in Improving Adult Literacy and Numeracy 2009', HC 19

Public Accounts Committee 'Department for Transport: The Failure of Metronet 2010', HC 390

Public Expenditure White Paper, 'Public Expenditure to 1979-80' 1976 Cmnd 6393

Public Sector Employment Trends 2005, ONS

Regional analysis of public sector employment, Economic and Labour Market Review September 2009

Regional, sub-regional and local gross value added 2009, December 2009 Statistical Bulletin, ONS

Research on the Effects of Fiscal Stimulus: Symposium Summary, FRSB Economic Letter, July 2008

Reinhart, C. M and Rogoff, K. (2009) 'This Time is Different: Eight Centuries of Financial Folly', New York, Princeton University Press

Roll, E. (1995) 'Where Did We Go Wrong? From the Gold Standard to Europe', London, Faber & Faber

Rubinstein, W. D. (1994) 'Capitalism, Culture and Decline in Britain, 1750–1990', London, Routledge

Russek, F. 'Did the 2008 Tax Rebates Stimulate Short Term Growth?', Congressional Budget Office Brief, June 2009

Sargent, T. J. and Wallace, N. (1981) 'Some Unpleasant Monetarist Arithmetic', in Federal Reserve Bank of Minneapolis Quarterly Review 1981

Schuknecht, L. von Hagen, J. and Wolswijk, G., (2008) 'Government Risk Premiums in the Bond Market: EMU and Canada', ECB

Tanzi, V. and Schuknecht, L. (2000) 'Public Spending in the 20th Century: a Global Perspective', Cambridge, CUP

Taylor, A. J. P. (1965) 'English History, 1914-45', Oxford, OUP

Thomas, B. (1936) 'Monetary Policy and the Crises: A Study of Swedish Experience' London, George Routledge & Sons

Timmins, N. (1996) 'The Five Giants: a Biography of the Welfare State', London, Fontana Press

Understanding Government Output and Productivity, ONS (2003)

Veblen, T. (1899) ' The Theory of the Leisure Class', republished Cosimo, 2007

Wiener, M. (1981) 'English Culture and the Decline of the Industrial Spirit', Cambridge, CUP

Wolf, A. (2001) 'Does Education Matter? Myths about Education and Economic Growth' London, Penguin Books

Wolf, A. (2010) 'More Than We Bargained For: the Social and Economic Costs of National Wage Bargaining', London, CentreForum

Index

Lightning Source UK Ltd.
Milton Keynes UK
14 January 2011
165711UK00001B/159/P